Securing the Faithful

Preventing and addressing crime in places of worship.

By Rick Arrington, CPS, NCPS II

SUNSET INSTITUTE PRESS

3710 34th Street • Lubbock, Texas • 79410
800-687-2121 • www.extensionschool.com

Securing The Faithful
©Sunset Institute Press

Copyright © 09/2015
All rights reserved.

Printed in the United States of America.

Cover Design: Richard Cravy
Formatting: Virgil Yocham

ISBN: 978-1-938335-68-6

And the tree of the field shall yield her fruit, and the earth shall yield her increase, *and they shall be safe in their land, and shall know that I am the LORD*, when I have broken the bands of their yoke, and delivered them out of the hand of those that served themselves of them.

Ezekiel 34:27

About the Author

Rick Arrington obeyed the Gospel in 1989 and has served in various teaching, and other roles since. Currently he serves as a shepherd (elder) with the church in Virginia. He has been married to Teresa, whose father was instrumental in his obedience to the gospel, for over 30 years. They have two adult children. A former Military Policeman, Rick served for over 25 years in various capacities at the City of Roanoke, Virginia Police Department, retiring as a Zone Commander of the Southeast Quadrant of the city. He has a BS in Criminal Justice, is a graduate of the Administrative Officer's Management Program at North Carolina State University, and has an extensive history in crime prevention. He currently is employed in Virginia where he is considered a subject matter expert in the field of crime prevention. He has developed and taught numerous new crime prevention courses for citizens, schools, law enforcement, planners and a host of other professions. Arrington began the Crime Prevention Through Environmental Design (CPTED) committee, which later evolved into Virginia's Safer By Design Coalition. Arrington is a Virginia certified Crime Prevention Specialist and was the fourth in the nation to be certified at the highest national level, National Crime Prevention Specialist II.

After the terrorist attacks on September 11, 2001, Mr. Arrington drew on his knowledge and experience and created an interactive computer-based instrument (ARMOR) to assist crime prevention practitioners in conducting security assessments in a number of different facilities. He also developed an instrument and training for the Bureau of Indian Education which was used to evaluate the vulnerability of over 6,000 tribal schools.

In 2006 Arrington and others created a comprehensive three day training course for law enforcement and faith organizations entitled, "Securing the Faith-Based Community." The course was replicated in several communities and a shortened one-day version was later developed and has been presented at several churches of Christ and other Faith-Based Organizations and meetings. Rick has applied his knowledge of crime prevention to service of the church in assisting in policy and planning for the Virginia Christian Camp and with providing individual input to Elders and Ministers in numerous churches. He has presented and assisted in security at various Protestant denominations, a Jewish Temple, Christian schools and has presented as a panel member at "Polishing the Pulpit," an annual conference for leaders and members of the church of Christ.

In 2007, he published a text entitled, Crime Prevention-A Law Enforcement Officer's Practical Guide, (Jones and Bartlett Publishers) which is currently being used by many in the proactive policing field as their desk reference to crime prevention issues and as basic crime prevention course text.

Rick has published articles on safe design, senior crime prevention, conducting security survey assessments on school facilities and numerous other crime prevention topics. Currently Rick serves as one of ten members on the newly created National Law Enforcement Committee to address metal theft.

Due to his extensive experience in prevention and his love of the church, he remains one of the "go to" people in Virginia's crime prevention field for questions pertaining to securing the faith community.

Table of Contents

Recent Headlines....

Two arrested in shooting death of Liberty City pastor

Lance Dixon and Monica Disare, The Miami Herald June 12, 2014

Two men, ages 19 and 20, have been arrested in the shooting death of Pastor Kenneth Johnson. Pastor Kenneth Johnson was on his way home when he got a phone call to return to his Liberty City church to give a helping hand.

Source: http://www.miamiherald.com/2014/07/11/4230664/liberty-city-minister-shot-killed.html#storylink=cpy

11-year-old shot in church parking lot

Posted: Jul 10, 2014 1:00 AM EDT Updated: Jul 17, 2014 1:00 AM EDT

HARRODSBURG, KY (WAVE) - An 11-year-old girl was shot in a church parking lot in Harrodsburg and police said the shooting was not an accident.

Source: http://www.wave3.com/story/25982602/11-year-old-shot-in-church-parking-lot

Church shooting details released

Bianca Cain Johnson and Valerie Rowell Friday, Aug 15, 2014

William "Bill" Rountree DaVitte was fatally shot at Marvin United Methodist Church about 10:30 Thursday night. A suspect was later arrested in Jacksonville, Fla. Florida authorities captured a Jacksonville man early Friday suspected in a shooting Thursday night that killed a Martinez man and injured his wife.

Source: http://chronicle.augusta.com/news/crime-courts/2014-08-15/church-shooting-details-released

Church shooting suspect Dylann Roof captured amid hate crime investigation

June 18, 2015 By Robert Costa, Lindsey Bever, J. Freedom du Lac and Sari Horwitz

Source: http://www.washingtonpost.com/news/morning-mix/wp/2015/06/17/white-gunman-sought-in-shooting-at-historic-charleston-african-ame-church/

Introduction

*The LORD is my shepherd; I shall not want. He maketh
me to lie down in green pastures: he leadeth me beside
the still waters.   He restoreth my soul: he leadeth me in
the paths of righteousness for his name's sake. Yea,
though I walk through the valley of the shadow of death, I
will fear no evil: for thou art with me; thy rod and thy staff
they comfort me. (Psalms 23:1-4)*

he four verses so often quoted and so well
known speak to the protective nature of the
shepherd. The picture of shepherd aptly also
fits the role of the elder of the church in providing
protection. Protection for the sake of the flock's soul but
also of the flock while
in the sheepfold. In
the old and new
testament we saw
how the Lord
delivered his people
when others served
themselves of them.
Is it inappropriate

> *"While we are zealously
> performing the duties of good
> citizens and soldiers, we certainly
> ought not to be inattentive to the
> higher duties of religion. To the
> distinguished character of
> Patriot, it should be our highest
> glory to add the more
> distinguished character of
> Christian." -George Washington*

then that the church today looks at how it might
prepare for the persecution of Christians? Should we

not take steps to prepare for crisis, to prevent violence and to secure the faithful?

The place of worship has long been considered off-limits to all but the most hardened of criminals. The most complete statistics that measure violence in places of worship are those tracked by Mr. Carl Chinn. The F.B.I. Uniform Crime Report and Incident Based Reporting do not separate out attacks by location as a faith-based organization. While Mr Chinn's statistics are the best we have by most accounts they under represent the scope of the problem. Still yet his data reports that between 1999 and 2014 there were 781 deadly force incidents at Faith-Based Organizations in the United States. About 37% of those or 289 resulted in the death of someone other than the attacker.[1] We truly live in a dangerous and changing world for faithful Christians. The question becomes one of why the increase in attacks at faith organizations? What is the motivation for violent attacks at the church? The answer is as Solomon said, "The thing that hath been, it is that which shall be; and that which is done is that which shall be done: and there is no new thing under the sun." The wicked have always attacked God's people for their own gain and it is no different today.

---

1. www.carlchinn.com Church Security Concepts

The true difference is that we in the United States are now seeing it on our shores and in our free land. Our founders honored God and were guided by his precepts but we have become weak as we allow the influence of God to be removed from our daily lives. Yes we must take steps to provide protection for the assembly. If we do our part surely god will do his.

On September 11, 2001 the United States was attacked by International Terrorist. Years before 2001, churches were attacked by Domestic Terrorists of various types. After the attacks in 2001 the U.S. Department of State indicated that terrorists from abroad often attack us based upon our different ideology, religious beliefs and even our economic power and influence. Domestic terrorists, such as the Ku Klux Klan and others also attack based upon ideology and religious beliefs. The one thing that both types of terrorists have in common is that they want their agenda and viewpoint publicized. Consider how quickly terrorists want to claim responsibility for mass killing events.

Nothing is so open and so recognizable as faith organizations.

SECURING THE FAITHFUL

There has long been a saying in the world of news media that says, "if it bleeds, it leads." Some years ago two people being killed would be huge news but today, mass murders barely get a blurb on the evening news unless one can link it to terrorism or an organization's agenda. Since September 2001 the previously sought after targets have been hardened, forcing the terrorists to seek new softer targets where larger assemblies may be present and where they can get media attention. This should concern faith organizations of all stripes. Nothing is so open and so recognizable as faith organizations. Huge crosses on the building, the Star of David and tall steeples quickly identify faith organizations.

The home grown groups may bring their own kind of trouble on the church. Consider the open stance of the church against abortion, against homosexuality, same sex marriage and any number of other topics. There are groups seeking to publicize their agenda and are willing to do so in a not so peaceful way. Is the church prepared to address such issues? What about the sole radical in an otherwise peaceful group that has taken it upon himself to eradicate the preacher who spoke against the topic?

SECURING THE FAITHFUL

Finally, we live in a time of violence, a time where everyone wants their few minutes of fame, even if they need die at the end of it. We live in a world that needs the church more than ever. Even though taxes are paid to provide for needs and necessities it is the church that ultimately ends up with the task of feeding, counseling, providing clothing and assisting in countless other ways. Some recent statistics have estimated that churches provide about half of the total or all volunteers in the United States. With all of these factors in play is there any doubt that the church needs to begin the work of preparing for violence? While there is no guarantee or way of preventing all attacks, it is my hope that I can provide some insight into methods to prevent attacks and also to address them appropriately if they come.

The Violent Attacker

The wicked have drawn out the sword, and have bent their bow, to cast down the poor and needy, and to slay such as be of upright conversation. (Psalms 37:14)

The terrorist attacker will be addressed later in crisis planning techniques. Their mindset is driven largely by publicizing their cause and attacking the beliefs of a faith. What I want to focus on here is the more probable encounters of the local church. Based upon the statistics mentioned earlier, certain triggers have been isolated that have led up to violence. From a planning standpoint understanding the likely triggers, the instrumentalities of the crime, and profile of the attacker from past events can go a long way to preventing an attack. Chinn's report noted that the top three known triggers for violent attackers were; robbery (23.9%), domestic relationship spillover (16.7%) and personal conflict or disagreement that were not based on relationships (13.8%). Gang activity and mental illness were tied for fourth place at 10.4% each. Let's consider the trigger events mentioned above for a moment.

Robbery

United States congregations of faith organizations generate an annual revenue of some 80 billion dollars. We should remember though that the majority of congregations in the Unites States are made up of less than 100 members. Most small congregations are unlikely to be targeted for robbery.

Robbery by definition is taking property by force or fear of force, with or without a weapon and not simply stealing. Congregations that are large and take in thousands of dollars in each offering are most likely those that would be targeted for robbery. Robbery is one of the simplest crimes to protect against. Good cash handling policies, use of private safe rooms for counting with multiple counters, use of a safe until deposits can be made, varying route for deposits and ensuring that no one person makes the deposit alone are simple practices that can reduce the probability of robbery resulting in violence. A caution that is often overlooked is the practice of publicizing contribution amounts via posting on a offering board, posting in the bulletin, and reporting on the website. If reporting to the congregation is the desired purpose of posting, and in most cases it is, then it is possible to set up a password protected page on the website for members only to see the contribution record.

Alternatively, verbally announcing it at the Sunday night service when only members are likely to be in attendance may provide some protection. Criminologists recognize that one thing which can contribute to prevention of theft is reducing or removing the motivating reward, in this case cash. Some churches are now accepting credit cards as well. The finally suggestion is the use of actual trained security staff. Later, I will be discussing a security team. The team is different from a professional security officer contracted for protecting funds until deposited.

Domestic Spillover

The statistics mentioned above interestingly demonstrate that 91.6% of the attackers were male. Male victims killed were 63.6% of the total. About 24% of the attackers were known to the ministry in some fashion. Over 72% of the violent attacks were perpetrated by a single attacker versus multiple attackers.

Statistics from the F.B.I. concerning hostages taken report that between 75% and 90% of hostage situations were domestic related.

The church is likely to encounter domestic violence for numerous reasons. First, in some cases the victim spouse may have been removed from the home and located in a safe shelter. It is often reported to the employer of the victim that the offender spouse is not to be allowed into the workplace. The offender knows one certain location, day and time to find the spouse, church services. Another reason that domestic situations find their way to the church is that the Minister may have been counseling the victim spouse and the offender blames the Minister for his spouse leaving him. In their angry state they begin to conceive reasons why their spouse left and their wrath turns to the Minister and the spouse. In some cases they blame the entire church. For example if the offender spouse is harming the victim, and both are members of the church, church discipline may result. These cases are the most difficult to protect against as the offender knows the protocols of the church, knows the layout of the building and even may know the home addresses, or have access to them, of members. The statistics perhaps even indicate this very type of scenario (domestic violence) in that over 67% of the incidents occurred outside the facility on ministry property. One might see how a domestic situation was reported to leadership and thus resulted in watching for the potential offender spouse and not allowing him/her in would provide prevention. The offender might then see their answer in meeting the spouse as they arrived on the property before entering the church building.

Understanding the statistics above, we must see that the key, regarding domestic spillover, is knowledge of the potential. Congregants should be encouraged to inform leadership or a designated person of any such conflict with spouses or others, and a plan to protect the individual and the congregation from violence be devised and implemented. Simple steps such as moving the potential victim to a different location than would be their normal seat or classroom may be helpful. Arranging for the member to be picked up so that their car would not be observed in the parking lot is another possibility, and of course their worshipping elsewhere for a time until cooler heads can prevail would be an option.

Shepherds need to be aware of what is going on in the lives of the sheep. For example a new convert may have a spouse or family member that strongly resents the church leading the family member to Christ because it does not follow their own family religious "tradition." A person who was disciplined by the church some time back may return for revenge, blaming the church for problems following their discipline. Members who are on certain medications and unable to obtain them or those that decide to self wean from medications may act out violently. Finally, as the shepherd would be watchful for dangers, so must the leadership be aware of environmental dangers. News of churches being targeted for this attack or that might be random and the church must take actions to protect members from any copycat or random selection also. The day following the shootings in the church in South Carolina a man showed up at a Richmond, Virginia faith organization wielding a weapon and yelling racial slurs as he beat on doors that were locked. In short the leadership must remain vigilant and aware!

As for dealing with the offender himself, I will recommend that this be the role of the Security Team, discussed later.

Personal Conflict

Conflict is not unusual, even in the church. (Acts 15:36-40) It is how the conflict is managed that is important. Many that we encounter in the church are not members of the church but rather may be recipients of services of the church. The church is often involved in benevolent services, and rightly so. Jesus said, "For I was an hungred, and ye gave me meat: I was thirsty,

12

and ye gave me drink: I was a stranger, and ye took me in: Naked, and ye clothed me: I was sick, and ye visited me: I was in prison, and ye came unto me." (Matthew 25:35-36) In this, he indicated the proper treatment of others and the proper attitude. Faith organizations are often involved in the following works:

- Providing food pantries,
- Providing clothing pantries,
- Providing shelter,
- Assisting with financial needs,
- Providing prison/jail ministries,
- Assisting in home visits to identify needs and to study the Bible,
- Providing financial, spiritual and marital counseling.

Few faith organizations are not involved in at least one of these activities that will bring persons to the facility. Now consider those that are most likely the recipients of this help. They are most likely; poor or needy, lonely or isolated, homeless, recently released from incarceration, emotionally in need, mentally ill, or substance abusers.

So, is the answer to abandon the benevolent works of the church and the outreach? God forbid! Surely we know that we are not even to discriminate against them, they are to be treated as brothers and sisters if obedient Christians. According to James, to discriminate against them or show favoritism to others is to blaspheme the name of Christ and to commit sin. (James 2:1-9) The issue then is how do we meet the obligation and do so safely? We know for the most part those that are poor or need a little help occasionally do not create concerns for safety but rather only certain ones cause us concern. Let's look specifically to the issue of homelessness because it encompasses several issues related to safety.

According to the U.S. Department of Housing and Urban Development, 2012 Point in Time Report, the homeless have a three times higher risk of death than the general population. The homeless population is very high in being substance abusers and second in suffering from mental illness. On top of that, 23% of the homeless population is considered chronically homeless. Most readers will already see the statistical link to mental illness and substance abuse. You will recall that Chinn's statistical data had mental illness in fourth as an attack trigger. Robbery can also be linked to substance abusers, seeking funding for their next fix. If we are to assist these in need, then it is crucial that members, or paid staff, be trained in crisis intervention techniques, conflict resolution and in recognizing certain signs of mental disorders.

We must always remember to show respect, even if it is someone we despise, as our example the "Good Samaritan" demonstrated. (Luke 10:30-37) Knowing how to communicate respectfully and kindly will go a long way toward preventing conflict with those we serve. Instructions that apply here are found in Proverbs 15:1, "A soft answer turneth away wrath: but grievous words stir up anger. Conflict that arises in the church or in an outreach program should lead us to consideration of the following resolution tools.

Conflict Resolution Tools/Training

Two Types of Conflict:

Realistic – That which is opposing in values, needs or interests.

Unrealistic – Opposition stems from error, ignorance, win/lose competitions, hostility, or need for tension release (Often associated with emotions).

▶ Anger, Distrust, Defensiveness, Fear

Always Deal with emotions first—

Before being able to assist in resolving the "true" issue, the emotions must first be dealt with. This means giving the individual our complete attention, listen!

Often what we consider listening is not listening at all. Most of us listen in part while formulating our response and miss the entire point. It has been estimated that over 75% of verbal communication is ignored or not understood fully. While I will provide some tips below to effective diffusion of situations, time and space is not sufficient to point out the excellent work of those specializing in the skills of listening and communicating effectively. I would recommend the church at least consider purchasing a book written by Robert Bolton, Ph.D. and published first in 1979 by Simon & Schuster publishers entitled, People Skills; How to Assert Yourself, Listen to Others, and Resolve Conflicts. There are also plenty of training courses regarding proper verbal communications and de-escalation techniques commercially available if there is interest in that route of education.

Short of a full course, I recommend at least the following methods of de-escalation and addressing conflict.

3 Step Process

1. Treat all with respect!

> The "good Samaritan" showed respect, even though the injured was a person his people despised.
>
> "And he answering said, Thou shalt **love** the Lord thy God with all thy heart, and with all thy soul, and with all thy strength, and with all thy mind; and thy neighbour as thyself." (Luke 10)

Dos and don'ts —

√ Do make good eye contact (If in person)

√ Do monitor your tone of voice

√ Do monitor your body language

√ Don't take their words personally, ignore name calling

√ Don't dominate

√ Don't judge

√ Don't criticize with negative evaluation of the person

√ Don't threaten

√ Don't be tricked into arguing a moot point (See next point below)

√ Don't rob them of the right to be upset (NEVER

say CALM DOWN, Say instead, I see you are upset and I want to help you or I hear what you are saying however to help you ...)

> *Pleasant words are as an honeycomb, sweet to the soul, and health to the bones. (Proverbs 6:3)*
>
> *A soft answer turneth away wrath: but grievous words stir up anger. (Proverbs 15:1)*

2. Listen <u>until you understand</u> their side.

√ Don't interrupt,

√ Don't question excessively (LET THEM VENT-LISTEN)

√ Deal with one issue at a time

√ DON'T tell them your "similar story" they don't care! You are now diffusing the emotions and getting to the real issue.

√ Restate their view of why they are upset, such as you are angry because.... (This may mean

> *Wherefore, my beloved brethren, let every man be **swift to hear, slow to speak**, slow to wrath: (James 1:19)*

3. After experiencing their side, and being certain they have calmed down, state your needs/views in context of helping them. If a policy prohibits you from doing what they want (giving them a double portion or whatever) brainstorm with *them...GIVE THEM CHOICES.*

State the policy then state choices available to them, for example, "I am not allowed to ...what I can do is to let you speak to Elder Jones, who is authorized or if you like you can come back tomorrow and I will ...."

Finally, understand that if they are suffering from certain mental issues, you may not be able to address their personal conflict realistically through diffusion, and policy should dictate what is to be done next, in this situation. Policy should always include having others assist you (to be witnesses, to help in self protection to demonstrate to the subject with conflict that they have more than one person to encounter) but it should always be done respectfully and kept low key.

Notice what Solomon wrote—

"Two are better than one; because they have a good reward for their labour. For if they fall, the

one will lift up his fellow: but woe to him that is alone when he falleth; for he hath not another to help him up. Again, if two lie together, then they have heat: but how can one be warm alone? And if one prevail against him, two shall withstand him; and a threefold cord is not quickly broken." (Ecclesiastes 4:9-12)

It is always also good for the Security Team and for leadership to know the laws of their state pertaining to disruption of worship and other applicable laws. A quick trip to the library, or in many cases an online search, will provide all that is needed. For example, a quick search of Virginia laws reveal laws pertaining to intentionally damaging of churches specifically, trespassing on church property, carrying dangerous weapons into places of worship, carrying a concealed weapon with a permit into a place of worship and several others. In knowing the content of the law, the church may make pertinent decisions as to how to address those specific items, such as to call the police immediately or wait to see how the conflict resolution efforts work.

Consideration for Safety in Outreach

"For I was an hungred, and ye gave me meat: I was thirsty, and ye gave me drink: I was a stranger, and ye took me in: Naked, and ye clothed me: I was sick, and ye visited me: I was in prison, and ye came unto me." (Matthew 25:35-36)

According to research, Faith-Based Institutions engage 45 million volunteers, nearly half of the total of all volunteers in America.[2] This should come as no surprise since faith organizations engage in; providing food pantries, clothing pantries, shelter, disaster relief, assist with financial needs, provide prison ministries, engage in home visits to identify needs and provide counseling and study opportunities. etc. Consider who it is that are most often served in these benevolent programs. Often they are the poor or needy, lonely or isolated, homeless, prisoners or recently released from jail, mentally ill and current or past substance abusers. Most religious organizations do not to discriminate or show favoritism. The issue then is how do we meet the mission of benevolence while doing so safely? Certainly we know that, for the most part,

---

2 America's Religious Congregations: Contribution to Society. November 2000. Independent Sector, http://www.independentsector.org/uploads/Resources/americas_religious_congregations.pdf

those that are poor or need a little help occasionally do not create the concerns for safety. There are however those individuals that do cause concern for the workers.

A report from the U.S. Department of Housing and Urban Development provides some interesting insight into those that might be served by the church in benevolent programs.[3] According to this report in 2012, the homeless population was high in the number substance abusers and second highest percentage was the severely mental ill. About 23% of the homeless were considered chronically homeless. You will recall that the number one trigger for violence at churches was robbery. Statistics from the Independent Sector, mentioned earlier, also noted that U.S. faith congregations generate an estimated $81 billion annually in revenues, much of which is used to support programs that address social needs. The motivation for robbery is cash or items that can be quickly converted to cash.

Additionally, other triggers for the violence that plagues religious bodies were personal conflict, domestic spillover, mental illness and drug abuse. Logically it follows that outreach workers providing services will encounter the home-

---

3 US Dept. of HUD 2012 Point in Time Report, Also,
www.clarityhumanservices.com

less, many of which will either be suffering from mental issues or substance abuse. Without funding for medication, many will be unstable and the outreach workers face numerous hazardous both on church property and in field services, such as home visits. It follows that in our attempt to Secure the Faithful, we must protect the outreach worker as well.

Three Steps to Protect in Outreach

In that most benevolent programs are staffed on-site by volunteers and church staff, it stands to reason that basically three measures will aid in keeping the workers safe. The three steps are:

– On-site Screening
– Policy and Training Development
– Individual Responsibility

Each of these steps will be addressed in more detail hereafter. Obviously, leadership must be engaged and participating in implementing any of these safety measures with the exception of Individual Responsibility. Maintaining safety in outreach is no less important than protecting the property and the assembly.

On-site Screening

Often the benevolent activities of the church are event oriented. For example, prior to cold weather the church may have a coat drive. In some cases the event may be a regularly scheduled event, such as one day per week opening a food closet or distribution center. In either case those that come will frequently be strangers to those volunteering to assist at the event.

We tell our children that a stranger is someone that you don't know well. That description applies here as well. We may serve the same person week after week but if they come only for the food and, there are lots of others coming, we rarely get to actually know the people. The necessity to move the line along becomes the priority. Since we do not know those seeking the assistance, we are not sure of the mental or emotional state of the individual. We are unaware of their addictions or other problems that might force irrational behavior and which might better enable us to minister to their specific need. Therefore, I recommend on-site screening of participants in these events.

Screening will serve two purposes; first, it will allow volunteers or staff to get to know those being served and second, it will provide an opportunity to read the individual and to evaluate their potential for violence.

Process, Method and Purpose

The suggested process will involve the creation of a "check-in station" set away from the area where the distribution may be conducted. For example, the church may set a table in the vestibule at the entrance of the location in which the distribution is conducted. Ideally the station should be outside the main facility or at least outside the area of distribution and in close proximity to another private room that may be needed for counseling or private diffusing of situations. Setting the screening in this fashion creates the funneling, or layered, effect that is desired to prevent persons from sneaking through or forcing their way in. Funneling may be provided by stanchions, ropes and other methods as well. (Think bank lines, amusement parks etc.) This also isolates any trouble away from those being served already. We are trying to avoid an audience that fuels the problem and endangers more people. In brief, we are addressing the issue of "crowd psychology." Much study has been done toward understanding the creation of mob behavior and how a group forms into an angry mob and this separation is designed to avoid certain factors leading to the polarization of such groups. Additionally, there should be adequate stations and staff to briefly screen the individuals without any irritating delays. Remember, even though they are receiving benevolence, nobody likes to stand and wait in a line unnecessarily.

It is <u>very important</u> that signage be posted with the <u>expected behaviors noted</u> such as; check-in requirements, how often they may participate, prohibited use of cigarettes and/or profanity on premises, times and days of operations and consequences of violating the prohibited behaviors. The posted information must be adhered to by staff and volunteers including times of opening and closing. Consider that the primary purpose is to screen but we must also avoid creating unnecessary conflict, thus starting on-time and avoiding the appearance of favoritism by letting some in early or after posted hours is crucial.

In most studies it has been suggested that over 70-80% of communication is linked to body language. Therefore screening individuals for body language and verbal indicators of violence will go a long way to preventing violence through early intervention.

The suggested method of screening is to use a ticket process. The individual gives the screener their name and other information that the church requires (i.e. where they last slept, other needs the church may have). The questions should be few and brief to avoid embarrassment and delaying the movement of the individuals in line. To reiterate, nobody likes standing in a slow or non-moving line. The screener should be provided training to observe behaviors that are not "normal" for the group as a whole or that indicate the potential for violence including verbal and non-verbal indicators. Some indicators of violence are listed hereafter.

The screener should also attempt to detect alcohol on the visitor's breath and indicators of substance use at that time. The workers must be provided guidance in what actions to take if an indicator of such is detected. For example, if a person smells of alcohol, a directive may require the worker to signal a staff person to take them aside and inform them that they can't enter because of the rule prohibiting persons that have consumed alcohol, but if the individual will tell them what is needed they will get the items for them this time. They might be informed that they will not be allowed in or served at all in the future if they return in this condition again. This serves the needs while also protecting others and informing the individual of consequences. In other words, it diffuses a potential hostile situation. Now for a moment consider if the screener says to the person, "You have to leave we don't serve anyone drunk." Would there likely be a different outcome?

Volunteers and Staff must Be Trained as to What Actions to Take If Individuals Become Violent at Their Suggestions. They must Be Trained That If They Provide the Items Requested, as Described Earlier, and the Individual Becomes Vocal but Is Leaving, Let Them Go Without Response! The Need of People to Have the Last Word Is the Cause of Many Violent Confrontations That Do Not End Well.

Another method of dealing with a potentially violent person, due to an identified behavior violation is to allow them to be served. If a single behavior is detected indicating a violent tendency, it may mean nothing. The more violent behaviors observed, the more attention should be given. In order to avoid embarrassment of an individual, and yet still alert the other workers of the potential violence, the church may opt to use a colored ticket system. All to be served that are checked in would be required to show a ticket at service. Various colored tickets might be used to alert others of potential without the individual being any the wiser.

Some indicators of potential for violence are:

- Threatening statements
- Intimidating, belligerent, or challenging behavior
- Being confrontational
- Demonstrating anger or agitated behavior
- Indicating feelings of persecution
- Blaming others
- Severe changes in mood while waiting
- Substance abuse
- Indication or comments of severe recent personal stress (e.g., recent lost job, home foreclosed, divorce, death of loved one, pending court or jail sentence and so on)

- Physical fight preparation (e.g., clinching their fists, wringing their hands, or squaring their lower body stance)

- Voice indicators (e.g., increase in pitch, nervous laugh or inappropriate laugh, speaking of a person as though they are not there-for example "she doesn't know who she is dealing with")

Policy and Training Development

Closely linked to the screening process is the need to train workers in what to do before crucial situations arise. Creation of policies in written form is the best method of providing standardized and consistent guidance regarding specific instances or situations.

One of the most important skills workers can develop is people skills. Many universities, consultant groups and even mental health agencies offer training in developing these skills. The skills will aid in diffusing potential hostile situations, identifying specific methods of addressing mental illness and even aid in outreach for the church in evangelism.

Church leadership should identify the need for such training, versus the potential harm from not having such training. If the church has members that are skilled in conflict resolution techniques, these may be offered at a minimum within the church family. The scripture suggests some food for thought on how to address such situations.

But the wisdom that is from above is first pure, then peaceable, gentle, and easy to be intreated, full of mercy and good fruits, without partiality, and without hypocrisy. (James 3:17)

Remember also that the fruit of the Spirit is love, joy, peace, longsuffering, gentleness, goodness, faith, meekness, and temperance. (Galatians 5:22-23)

Through creation of policies we can guide members, staff and volunteers toward a peaceable end, while demonstrating obedience and love in benevolence.

Individual Responsibility

The great commission told Christians to go, teach and make disciples. This of course involves leaving the building, although we all suffer from a bout of "pewitis" now and again. Guidance through training or policy should be provided the field workers, or at least offered, to ensure their safety as they conduct bible studies, counsel, visit and so on.

The best advice for safety in these endeavors is that which was given long ago but still applies today, <u>don't go alone</u>. The reasons are even explained in scripture...

> *"at the mouth of two witnesses, or at the mouth of three witnesses, shall the matter be established."* (Deut. 19:15, 2 Cor. 13:1) Christ provided the example himself. *"And he called unto him the twelve, and began to send them forth by two and two..."* (Mark 6:7)

In pairs, new Christians with the experienced worker may learn to handle unsafe situations, and having witnesses will protect the reputation of individuals from false accusations. Criminologists understand that anything that increases the effort for the criminal to be successful will go a long way toward preventing the attack; two are harder to attack than one.

The church leadership cannot provide everything to protect members. Some of the protection comes from common sense and acceptance of personal responsibility. The church should give guidance but the individual should take personal responsibility as well.

Some Suggestions For Visiting

— Never visit anyone alone that is suspected of being unstable. If one knows the person to be visited is suspected of being unstable it is a must that others accompany them. Little good can come of a visit full of false accusations, innuendo or physical violence. Even if you are capable of dealing with the violence, what harm might the visit bring to the reputation of the church?

— If one *must* make a visit on their own with stable persons, they need take steps to protect themselves from harm. Many of the steps below are provided to allow the worker reaction time. The potential harm might not be from the individual being visited but may come from a hostile spouse, others in the neighborhood or in efforts to rob the worker or others.

— Let someone know where you are going and when you will return. In some cases a worker may even wish to tell the visited person that they can't stay long because they are expected back at a certain time.

— Charge your cell phone and have it ready for an emergency call.

— Park one house away and walk up then listen before knocking. Police officers have done this for years when responding to one of the most dangerous types of calls encountered-the domestic argument. By parking away from the house you may be able to observe trouble prior to approaching. If a hasty retreat is necessary the car is out of the immediate danger area. In listening before knocking the individual must resolve that if they hear fighting, yelling and arguing, or items being broken that they will return to their car, lock the doors, start the car and then call police or others for assistance.

— Once you have left your car and are approaching the home, place your car keys in a quickly accessible pocket or location. If one must flee, digging in a huge purse for keys in unacceptable.

— If weather permits, ask to sit on the porch to talk. It is a fact that one is safer in an open clearly visible area.

— If invited inside, choose a seat near the door for a quick exit.

— Don't accept any food or drink that is not sealed.

— Trust your instinct and if you feel uneasy, make an excuse and depart. God has provided us with instinct. It is that instinct that makes one feel uncomfortable at certain places, around certain people, and in certain situations. Trust what God has provided, it is our alarm!

Protecting the Assembled

"The art of war teaches us to rely not on the likelihood of the enemy's not coming, but on our own readiness to receive him; not on the chance of his not attacking, but rather on the fact that we have made our position unassailable." –Sun Tzu, The Art of War

It may seem odd to provide a quote from *The Art of War* but the point is to emphasize that to protect the assembled at church services and functions on the property we must prepare. Clearly all Christians would recognize the teachings of the scriptures to be beneficial for both our spiritual and our physical life as well. *"According as his divine power hath given unto us all things that pertain unto life and godliness, through the knowledge of him that hath called us to glory and virtue ..."* (2 Peter 1:3) Therefore, the most important thing that we can do to prevent or mitigate attacks is to prepare. The F.B.I. used to teach a method of running through scenarios in your brain with all sorts of twists and turns so that whatever the incident, it would have been thought of prior in case it ever occurred. The idea was that if one "pre-thought" the actions the actions would come quicker, they called this "mental mapping."

I am not suggesting that all of the congregation think this through but rather I am suggesting that the congregation do as they were told in Acts 6 concerning the widows and orphans, look out among your congregation and "identify men." Identify men who are capable of taking on the task of being part of a Security Team. In Acts they were looking for certain qualifications for a certain task. This team also must have certain skills and qualifications. Just as we discussed previously, we do not want arrogant, prideful, hot heads for this task, neither do we want the very timid, indecisive types.

Many churches select a Team Leader who leads in the tasks to be assigned and also in selecting others. Ideally, if your congregation has law enforcement officers, recent military, or security professionals who have had lots of training in diffusion situations, they would make good team leaders. A key factor by necessity must be faithful attendance. Ultimately church leaders must decide; the size of the team, what the focus should be, the approval process for issues to be addressed and whether team members that are authorized to carry concealed weapons will be permitted to do so. (We will discuss the point of weapons and conceal carry permits shortly.)

SECURING THE FAITHFUL

The duties of the security team are primarily to; draft plans to prevent crime and violence, draft security policies, provide security during assembled events, and assist with developing crisis plans. The security team or Team Leader will likely provide, or provide for, training as needed to the congregations for visitation in the community, outreach programs, large events management and all security related activities.

The Security Team

"For by wise counsel thou shalt make thy war: and in multitude of counsellors there is safety." (Proverbs 24:6)

Tbe size and scope of the security team will absolutely vary from congregation to congregation. Occasionally extra temporary assistance from members may be needed for special events where specific trouble might be expected or where a sizeable crowd is expected.

We have already identified to some degree the makeup of the team. In addition to developing security plans, overseeing the physical facility safety and aiding or in or actually developing crisis plans, this team will be training others as well. This team may, as a last resort to mitigate harm or injury, have to physically intervene and

> *"For scarcely for a righteous man will one die: yet peradventure for a good man some would even dare to die."*

must be prepared to do so. Finding out that a team member is not capable mentally or physically at the time of need is simply not acceptable. Every effort must be made to ensure their willingness and capability even to endure self harm and possibly even death to save the larger assembly. This is why the team members recommended were police officers and military, they have demonstrated their willingness.

The Question of Arms

Now to address the elephant in the room, guns. The statistics we have been looking at reveal that in the data regarding faith organization violent attack incidents, the primary weapon of use was a gun (58%), followed by a knife (17%). If the criminal is armed in these attacks, it seems to me that we would not want to bring a stick or hands only to a gun or knife fight. Having said that, there will always be people on both sides of the, arm or not arm discussion in the church. Since the New Testament church set in order leadership at each congregation, I believe it is the role of that leadership to determine how to handle this subject.

Each congregation will be different, the community they are located in will be different and no central governing body on earth should be directing the local congregation relative to this. I do not believe the scriptures address this topic directly, that is to say as to give direction from the inspired word. I am aware of scriptures some might point to on both sides but I see no "direct scriptural answer." As such, I will not recommend one or the other but leave the decision up to the local congregation and their leadership. I will provide my "personal opinion" (Not scriptural direction) on certain aspects and attempt to provide some information of use in making the decision.

I should state at the outset that I am a gun rights advocate. Rather than bore anyone with my arguments as to why I feel as I do I will go no further. I simply thought it best that the reader understands my personal feelings on the topic as they read, having said that, I will state unequivocally that I do not support guns openly carried in places of worship. I believe to carry openly detracts from the sense of safety and may force attendees to "think" that the church is less, rather than more, safe. This would not necessarily apply in a large event where off-duty uniformed police or security was hired and in which it would be common to see uniformed armed persons.

Now to the point of guns carried concealed or open. In an April 2014 interview gun rights advocate, author and Crime Prevention Research Center President John Lott stated, "With just one single exception, the attack on congresswoman Gabrielle Giffords in Tucson in

2011, every public shooting since at least 1950 in the U.S. in which more than three people have been killed has taken place where citizens are not allowed to carry guns."[4] You must conduct your own research into this to aid in your decision of allowing the Security Team to carry concealed or not.

From the understanding of the "rational choice theory" of situational crime prevention, which addresses how criminals select their targets, the less the perception of risk to the criminal and the more effort to carry out their crimes successfully are very much related to the selection of a criminal's target. That is to say, if there is an open perception that weapons are not allowed, they may be more likely to select the site for the attack rather than selecting another in which the risk is greater.

On the issue of concealed weapons permits, it should be noted that they are easy to obtain or no process at all required in most states. The current estimate of states that hold to a "shall issue" process is thirty-nine. That is thirty-nine require the permit be issued if applied for. Two require no permit to carry concealed weapons. In some states, one simply applies, and firing the weapon or quali-

---

4 http://cnsnews.com/mrctv-blog/matt-vespa/study-all-two-multiple-public-shootings-1950-took-place-where-guns-were-banned

fying on a firing range is not necessary. That being said, I would recommend that if the church opts to allow the team to carry concealed, they be required to prove proficiency with the weapon they carry annually, if for no other reason as a protection from liability.

If authorized to carry a weapon, training and written policies must also emphasize when the weapon may be used and must always emphasize that it is to be used only as a last resort. Other non-lethal weapons should be treated similarly with regard to researching from a liability standpoint, ensure training is completed and a policy of appropriate use be provided. Less than lethal weapons are generally; stun guns, tasers, and chemical or pepper sprays.

One issue that all churches must address with concealed carry permits and authorization is that many individuals now have concealed carry permits. Many members of the church may have a permit and simply choose to carry a weapon to church themselves, revealing that they are carrying the weapon to nobody. This poses a real problem in a critical incident for the Security Team.

A critical incident is always a chaotic event. The team may be handling the incident in accordance with protocol when the well-meaning member (not part of the

Security Team) draws his own weapon; introducing a di-
lemma to the team as to if the member is part of the attack. Needless to say, it may not end well. So what information is available to address this specific issue? Firearms laws in individual states may give you the authority
to prohibit firearms, even by those authorized to carry concealed with a permit. For example, Virginia law (§18.2-
283) states, that one may not carry a dangerous weapon
into a place of worship while a religious assembly is occurring without, "good and sufficient reason." Seems clear
enough until you start to ask, what is a good and sufficient
reason? In an opinion of Virginia's Attorney General, ren-
dered April 8, 2011, he declared that personal protection
was a "good and sufficient reason" but that churches may
ban the person from carrying a weapon into the assembly.[5] This essentially interprets the law to be that private
property owners may prohibit those carrying concealed to
do so on their property and a church is considered private
property. In fact the clarification says just that. Virginia's
concealed carry laws also note that having a permit does
not authorize the carrying neither into places that the law
prohibits, nor into places where private property owners
prohibit it.[6]

5http://www.oag.state.va.us/Opinions%20and%20Legal%20Resources/O
pinions/2011opns/11-043%20cole.pdf

6 Code of Virginia

Each congregation must research the laws of your state first, and in compliance, address this question. One way of avoiding the appearance of being a "soft target", yet having your authorized team being the only ones authorized to carry weapons is by use of signage, verbal announcements or a letter prohibiting persons with a permit from carrying concealed on church grounds.

Sample verbiage on a sign that might indicate the property is protected, but also avoid introducing strange firearms into an incident by those authorized to carry concealed is,

> *"We recognize the rights of individuals to carry firearms lawfully; however the church allows only persons authorized by the leadership which have been trained in security policies of the church to carry firearms within the facility. We have taken steps to protect the congregation and our visitors. We ask that, if armed, you secure your firearm in a locked compartment within your vehicle to enhance the security operations within the church."*

Alternatively the church may chose to authorize others to carry, but by signage request they make known to the Security Team the fact that they are carrying concealed.

In my opinion, there are two considerations– Scriptural and Safety. I believe that protecting God's people, even to the use of weapons may be argued to be scriptural. After all, David used a weapon to defeat Goliath on behalf of God's people. How many Egyptians were killed pursuing the Israelites? One Old Testament scripture that actually addresses justification for taking a life in self protection is found in Exodus 2:2, *"If a thief be found breaking up, and be smitten that he die, there shall no blood be shed for him."* The Psalmist wrote, *"Blessed be the LORD my strength, which teacheth my hands to war, and my fingers to fight:"* (Psalms 144:1) Again, I am providing fodder for consideration only.

Scripturally we must not only consider what is authorized but also we must consider the influence that it may have on the weaker brother. In Acts 4 when questioned about the authority to heal, the disciples were warned by their captors not to teach in the name of Jesus but Peter and John rightly answered (Verse 18-19), "whether it be right in the sight of God to hearken unto you more than unto God, judge ye." God's command always overrides any right the constitution gives me, if I am Christ's follower. He must have preeminence and rule in my life. (Col. 1:18)

I have a concealed carry permit but if it offends my brother to the point of causing him to stumble, leave the church, or hurts his faith, I choose not to carry it. *"But take heed lest by any means this liberty of yours become a* stumbling block to them that are weak." (1 Corinthians 8:9) "It is good neither to eat flesh, nor to drink wine, nor any thing whereby thy brother stumbleth, or is offended, or is made weak." (Romans 14:13-21) I hope that I have provided sufficient information for the hard decision regarding weapons being authorized by any in the church.

Specific Duties During Regular Assembly

The Security Team training must include specific duties and assignments. Team duties should include securing all doors that are not to be unlocked for access from outside. They may be part of the team that monitors the counting of the offering as well. As already mentioned team members must monitor the parking lots and entrances and must address issues as training and policy dictate. The team serves in the capacity that relates to the security of the church. The role may vary according to congregation size, locations and needs. In the next few paragraphs we will examine a primary role of the Security Team, the assembling of the saints.

Ideally all but one entrance will be secure in order to guide all persons arriving for the regular assembly through the same entrance and passed the team members assigned in that area. The team members are at this entrance to observe the parking lots and to screen arrivals for unusual behaviors, characteristics, clothing and carried

items. While one or two unusual behaviors or appearances may occur, they are not in and of themselves
cause for panic. They are cause for closer monitoring. As
the below described behaviors begin to mount, closer
scrutiny is warranted. Some examples of cause for closer
scrutiny may include:

1. Clothing that is out of the normal
    for the particular church environ-
    ment.

2. Clothing that is unusual for the
    weather conditions such as a
    heavy or long coat in warmer weather.

3. Carrying items not normally carried such as large
    backpacks. It should be noted that weapons may be
    concealed in a zippered bible case, purse or smaller
    items also. The team should become familiar with the
    "normal" appearance of such items. We do not advo-
    cate parcel searches. This is just to ensure closer
    scrutiny of persons with items that cause "concern."

Note the bible on the left indicates unusual weight and shape, not normal for a bible as with the photo on the right. Above shows the case open.

4. Especially dirty, soiled and offensive smelling clothing. Again, this is not a concern of its own but it may become one.

5. Unknown persons who sit in the parking area for extensive periods of time. This may be during the week when no services are underway. Could the person be watching the minister, the church activities, the secretary? The team may not be on premises and the police need be called to inquire into the activity.

6. Unknown persons in the parking area that appearing to be watching others. Often domestic quarrels find their way to the church and in some cases custody battles. This may be a non-custodial parent or an angry husband. It deems monitoring by the team.

7. Persons removing unusual, covered or concealed items from the vehicle, especially just before services begin. If the tem observes a man opening his trunk and lifting something covered but long, it could be a gun. This definitely would be an unusual occurrence for the services and warrant watching.

8. Unknown persons who sit in the parking area through the service as though waiting for someone. This

behavior should be closely monitored. It may be a person waiting for an individual to legitimately pick them up or to do them harm. Remember the church grounds are where most attacks occur.

9. Persons exiting their vehicle toward the church but leaving their vehicle running without any passengers within the vehicle. The obvious reason for this is that they intend to be leaving very shortly, perhaps fleeing.

10. Obvious attempts to not be noticed or greeted.

11. Loud and angered questioning of the Minister, accusations of "judging" and saying, "you will pay" or "you will be judged," etc.

12. Inquiring about the identity of the Minister, the Elders or specific persons.

13. Keeping their hand in their pocket, especially if only one hand and in warm weather.

14. Entering with others and one attempting to get greeters (Team Members) attention diverted with nonsense questions, asking to speak privately etc.

15. Wild eyed appearance with obvious agitation.

16. Becoming angry when asked normal questions such as, "are you just visiting today?"

17. Inappropriate laughing (often a sign of nervous-ness).

18. Intoxications, drugged appearance, confusion and signs of mental instability.

19. Signs of carrying a concealed weapon. Certain indicators of persons that are carrying concealed weapons have been observed going back many years by officers. This began by officers experimenting in large cities on spotting persons carrying concealed. Those who carry concealed weapons daily even are detectable with some of these indicators, especially when practiced. While these are not fool proof, and do take time to develop, they may warrant closer observation or other action. New technology does make carrying concealed weapons harder to detect but in most cases the only ones using the technology and devices for carrying are doing so as part of planned rational use. Attackers are rarely rational!

a. **Security Touch:** Often those carrying concealed weapons unconsciously touch the weapon to ensure it is still there or to adjust the weapon. This may be very subtle and difficult to see. It may not be with the hand alone. The individual may simple touch it with their elbow or hand. The best time to observe persons suspected of  Even with the jacket opened an indication of a weapon is detectable.

50

carrying a concealed weapon for the security touch is when changing levels such as going up or down stairs or seating or rising from a seated position. Weapons are generally heavy and shift in these occasions resulting in the check for security of the weapon. Test this by watching someone you know that carries a concealed weapon, such as a friend that is a Detective or one that has a concealed carry permit. You will start to see the behaviors.

b. **Clothing bulge or drooping:** A technique that is helpful in revealing concealed weapons in this fashion is to have one member greeting to the left of persons entering while another team observes. Most (not all) concealed weapons are likely to be on the right side waist area and thus the greeter shifts to force the person entering to twist their torso slightly which causes any weapon to be more visible as it protrudes slightly more than normal away from the twisted torso. As to the drooping clothing, those that may attempt to carry a weapon in their waistband or a pocket will display the obvious drooping of clothing.

c. **Unusual Walking:** In some cases person may attempt to carry long guns (shotguns, rifles etc.)

under a long coat or even in the leg of trousers. The result is that they walk unusual in trying to conceal the weapon or not bend at the needs due to the weapon restricting movement in the trouser. A shorter gait on one side may indicate an ankle holster or other weapon concealed near the ankle. This is extremely hard to detect but it suspected, closer scrutiny of the ankle area is warranted. Following the person in and locating yourself in an area that you may see their ankles when seated may confirm weapon suspicion. Please be aware and train staff that a disability may also cause an unusual walk.

d. **Observed Weapon:** Obviously there are cases where a weapon is simply observed. In some cases it may be a harmless visitor with a concealed carry permit but in others the would-be offender may just be sloppy or not have thought the concealment through.

The Security Team and leadership should have a plan in place to implement if a weapon is observed or suspected. Many things must be considered but a few come to mind immediately. If the weapon is detected in the parking lot or outside, should the person be approached outside before they have access to the larger crowd? In most cases the answer is yes, but circum-stances will dictate the action. If in the entrance hall, is there a technique of inviting the person to step aside or into another room for a question, and, if so what will the other team members do? If the weapon is detected and deemed to be carried legitimately, what steps will be taken? Should the team ask if they may secure it until after services or escort the individual to his car where he/she might secure it? The team should not "confiscate" or even use that word but rather offer to secure the weapon until after services. If this is an option the leadership chooses an individual must be trained to make the weapon safe and a secure location provided, such as a small gun safe. These are but a few of the questions posed by the concealed carry laws and question.

Security Plans, Procedures and Inspections

The Security Team Leader and members of the team should begin their work by developing certain plans, procedural policies and inspecting the physical environ-ment of the church properties.

Physical Environment Considerations

Expert consultants may be contacted to provide the church a security risk assessment for a fee. Under-standing that many smaller congregations do not have the re-sources to afford the thousands of dollars typically charged for security assessments, I suggest contacting your local law enforcement agency to see if they offer free security surveys or assessments. If so, churches should avail themselves of the service. It not only is a security need but also provides a great way to meet the law en-forcement officers that serve the congregation and maybe even evangelize a bit. Do not make the mistake that many do of assuming this service provided free by the police is substandard, it usually is not. I conducted a survey for a facility once that had paid a consultant over $8,000 to do and the facility manager told me that the survey document I gave them was much more comprehensive and useful. I did this when I was an officer and the survey was free.

I am providing a checklist hereafter that is the basis of a security assessment which may be used to examine the premises if no other options are available. Not being familiar with any of the churches that might use this instrument, I cannot assert that anything herein will create an absolute safe environment. The information is based upon my training and experience as a "Subject Matter Expert" in the field of crime prevention and things that are "typically seen" in these assessments. In addition, I have provided recommendations related to them. I have included this assessment in question and answer format, along with typical recommendations regarding each question. I am certain that the information is not all-inclusive but should provide a very basic guide in beginning to address the environmental issues that need to be addressed and considered for making the facility safer.

The list is broken down by the type of vulnerability it addresses and each question provides some information as to the importance of the item.

ROBBERY VULNERABILITIES

Church History and Policies

1. Has the church been robbery free or attempted robbery free over the last twelve months?

    ☐ Yes ☐ No ☐ N/A

In recent statistics robbery was the leading trigger cause of death in faith organizations. Perhaps the best indicator of vulnerability is the history of the church. While absence of robbery incidents does not indicate lack of vulnerabilities, churches that have been robbed within the past twelve months may have a higher chance of being robbed again. By examining the crime history at the particular facility we are able to gain a better understanding of what measures may need to be implemented, and to what degree, in order to reduce the potential for criminal acts.

2. Is the church located in a high crime area or an area with known crime generators?

☐ Yes ☐ No ☐ N/A

Churches are needed in all communities. The fact that a church is located in a high crime neighborhood, or one that is associated with increased crime, simply means that the church has to take additional steps to protect its employees and itself from loss. Proverbs 16:3 tells us that we are to, "Commit thy works unto the LORD, and thy thoughts shall be established." We are told by Jesus to go into all the world to preach the Gospel (Mark 16:15-16) and all includes poverty stricken communities, high crime communities and rich communities alike.

3. there a policy prohibiting opening any non-public access door to unauthorized persons?

   ☐ Yes ☐ No ☐ N/A

Robbers are not limited to public access when perpetrating their crimes. They may attempt entry to the back office area of a church using some ruse of injury or delivery need.

It is recommended that back door use be kept to a minimum and whenever possible, deliveries be made through the public access in churches. Ideally, mail will be picked up at the post office rather than delivered directly to the church. This addresses the potential of mail bombs as well as the vulnerability of robbery threats. When deliveries are accepted at back doors, specific hours for deliveries should be coordinated with the vendor to insure delivery is during times that more workers may be present and at times that do not interfere with church activities.

4. the church in a populated area, visible to businesses and/or homes?

   ☐ Yes ☐ No ☐ N/A

Robbers are apt to weigh their effort for success, reward and the potential for detection or capture. Being isolated is directly related to the amount of effort and their risk factor. Churches located in populated areas should take advantage of their neighbors and offer every opportunity for natural surveillance into the church. Churches that are located in isolated areas need to insure that they strengthen their security.

5. Is the church located away from access to Interstates or major highways?

    ☐ Yes ☐ No ☐ N/A

As mentioned above, the potential for success is key in the selection of a target by criminals, therefore, churches near quick escape routes such as interstate ramps and major highways have a higher potential for victimization, absent adequate prevention steps. Parking lot exit designs that require traffic to exit indirectly onto a secondary street or away from on-ramps go a long way toward making the church a less attractive target.

6. Does the church have a reputation for being busy (active) frequently?

    ☐ Yes ☐ No ☐ N/A

To the criminal mind, any person in the area represents a potential witness, which limits the probability of a successful robbery. Whatever steps can be taken to increase potential witnesses are steps well worth taking. Providing working space for volunteer groups while the Minister is there alone, allowing use by civic groups, scouts, and the like increase the risk of detection and make the criminal act more difficult, thus reducing the probability of a robbery while those individuals are present.

7. Is the church frequented by police patrols?

    ☐ Yes ☐ No ☐ N/A

Obviously where police patrols frequent there is a much less likely potential for crime problems of all kinds. Any incentive to draw officers to the church, especially during the weekday when fewer staff or members may be present, is encouraged. This may be done by; offering use of the office, a telephone, the restroom facility or simply making a request of the beat officers in the area to stop by and visit.

8. Are contributions counted by two individuals, not including the treasurer, who is responsible for deposits, in an isolated (preferably locked) room?

    ☐ Yes ☐ No ☐ N/A

Internal theft is an issue with this recommendation as well as robbery. Cash controls such as two counting (minimum), recording the amounts, and not including the person responsible for deposits in the count significantly reduce the potential for internal theft but also by isolating the counting and it being done by two, the effort is increased for the would-be robber.

9. Are all deposits made at irregular (non-routine) times and by non-routine routes by two persons?

☐ Yes ☐ No ☐ N/A

Routine allows for patterning and planning of robberies and it is discouraged. Irregular deposits at non-specific random times are recommended whenever possible. The use of two in the deposit encourages safety by creating additional effort for the robber, extra eyes to search for anything suspicious, reducing accusations of theft by those making deposits and improved witness potential in the event of an actual robbery.

10. Are there standardized procedures for reporting incidents to the police?

☐ Yes ☐ No ☐ N/A

All employees and members should be trained by the Security Team to contact them first unless an emergency occurs. Non-emergency reports to the police should be handled by the Security Team following church policy and protocol. Likewise, all members should be trained to report anything that is not normal for the particular church or event to the Team.

11. Does the church use a recorded serial number bill, marked money or other technique for identifying money stolen in a robbery?

☐ Yes ☐ No ☐ N/A

An investigative tool, the use of bait money or traceable bills could serve as a deterrent indirectly by insuring the capture of the robber. If robbery is determined to be a very real possibility, this may be a consideration for the church. The reputation of quick apprehension is bound to deter other criminals from seeing your church as an easy mark.

12. Is there a policy/procedure addressing how employees/members are to react during a robbery or other violent incident?

☐ Yes ☐ No ☐ N/A

All churches, subject to robbery, should have a policy concerning robberies and what specific action their employees should take during and after the robbery.

Training of money counters, and those making deposits should be based on this policy and the policy reviewed regularly to insure that they are aware of what is expected.

13. Is robbery prevention/response training provided to employees?

☐ Yes ☐ No ☐ N/A

As mentioned above, all employees, counters and those making deposits should be trained concerning specific hazards that they might encounter. Specifically they should be trained that once a robbery begins, they should assist the robber with whatever is requested, do or say nothing to upset the robber, and to cooperate fully. The ultimate goal should be to give the robber what they demand in order that the incident may end quickly and without harm. Robbery training should also

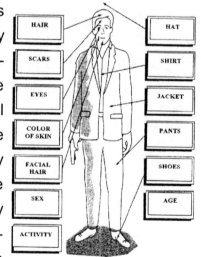

include that doors be locked as soon as the robber departs, police be called and Security Team Leader then called and to touch nothing until law enforcement arrives.

Training of employees or church volunteers handling money or most likely to be involved in a robbery should include concentrating on getting a good physical description of the robber for the police. Typically the best way to do this is to train to start from the head working downward.

14. If surveillance video is used, is there a policy specifying retention periods and cataloging of disks?

☐ Yes ☐ No ☐ N/A

 While surveillance video has more of an investigative role than preventative, it can assist law enforcement officers in identifying robbers, burglars and in identifying suspects of internal theft. Criminals frequently visit their target in advance of the criminal act to evaluate the risk and effort for success, and as such may be identified from recordings that are catalogued by date and retained for a minimal period, such as thirty days. Newer digital systems are easily stored and enhanced if needed. Extensive thought should be given as to the most strategic location for cameras. Cameras may be used not only to investigate robberies but also to combat false accusations about church misconduct. The video recording device should be secured to prevent removal, erasure or damage of the recording by unauthorized persons.

15. Does the church encourage members to identify crime problems and theft opportunities?

☐ Yes ☐ No ☐ N/A

Members should be trained as to the value of their role with the church, relative to security. We advocate an approach referred to as, "The Three R's." This approach involves the Security Team training all members about the first two R's and the Team handling the third R. The three R's are:

RECOGNIZE, REPORT and RESPOND.

In this approach members are trained to RECOGNIZE that which is suspicious. Specifically that which is unusual for the church, the activity, unusual behaviors, unusual clothing for the weather etc. Once it is recognized as unusual the members should REPORT the suspicious to the Security Team Leader or other member of the team to RESPOND appropriately.

Members should also be trained to report potential issues to the team. Things such as known domestic violence, separations or divorce that is less than ami-cable, persons not taking their prescribed medications that address mental anxiety, emotional depression, and anger and so on. Knowledge allows for planning and early interventions, if deemed needed. The clear reason that specifically identified persons should re-ceive the report is that they will be aware of the proper accepted response of the church, they will be respon-sible to maintain confidentiality as much as can be done without compromising safety, and by only have a few trusted and trained individuals, we avoid gossip.

As already indicated, after receiving the report, it is the Team leader or members that must RESPOND, in accordance which protocols that have already been developed in advance and are agreed upon by leadership. This will vary as each church develops policies and protocols.

16. Is there a zero tolerance policy for internal theft that involves measures to deter such theft?

☐ Yes ☐ No ☐ N/A

While we hope this is not a problem that any church experiences, it has been in the news before at some faith organizations and as such should be considered.

"And if any man will sue thee at the law, and take away thy coat, let him have thy cloak also." (Matthew 5:40) and *"Moreover if thy brother shall trespass against thee, go and*

> *tell him his fault between thee and him alone: if he shall hear thee, thou hast gained thy brother. But if he will not hear thee, then take with thee one or two more, that in the mouth of two or three witnesses every word may be established. And if he shall neglect to hear them, tell it unto the church: but if he neglect to hear the church, let him be unto thee as an heathen man and a publican."* (Matthew 18:15-17)

Policy is the deterrent and the tool for prosecution, if need be. Of course scriptural considerations must first be followed. A well stated theft policy identifying actions that may be taken is at the center of any such deterrence. Regardless of the existence of a policy relative to internal theft, it is recommended that a deterrent policy be drafted and include:

• Require different persons counting the offering than those depositing the funds,

• Require counters to document their total count in written form,

• Absent extenuating needs, do not have the church treasurer count the offering initially but rather count it for accuracy afterward,

• Require the treasurer provide monthly financial records and reports and that they be reviewed by leadership (or entire congregation as an alternative), and

- Order an annual independent audit of the books to avoid the possibility of impropriety.

Exterior

1. Are all parking areas for the auditorium visible from the vestibule?

☐ Yes ☐ No ☐ N/A

As much as is possible, the Security Team should be able to view the entire parking lot for any vehicle. Statistics cited earlier have demonstrated that close to 70% of the known violent attacks occurred outside on ministry property. The Security Team should be monitoring the parking area before and after services for any abnormal behavior, strangers, persons that have been barred for behavior or threats, persons exiting vehicles with weapons and then putting a coat on concealing the weapon etc. and they should have a plan to respond accordingly. Response plans must be developed and the team trained before any such incident. Such plans may include locking the doors, stopping people from going out until the person is addressed by police or some other method devised by the team. In most cases it is best to let the police interact with the individual rather than the team, not only for safety reasons but for liability concerns.

2. Are all concealment locations around the church limited or reduced through design, use or other means?

☐ Yes ☐ No ☐ N/A

Reducing the concealment locations around the church discourages attackers or robbers from waiting for an opportune moment to don a mask and enter the church or firing upon person from concealment.  Concealment locations can be limited by removal of foliage, large items and/or privacy fencing. By removing concealment the church is open to observation from casual passers and the robber's goal is much more difficult.

Are aesthetics more important than security?

3. Is lighting sufficient to insure facial recognition and provide visual surveillance both into and out of the church?

☐ Yes ☐ No ☐ N/A

The purpose of lighting is to enhance observation after dark, provide safety from stumbling and hazards, and to provide  some insulation from liability claims. There should be adequate lighting to prevent persons from concealing themselves in the shadows and to ensure safe walking.

There are many styles and types of lighting. Consideration is usually given to efficiency first but should also address color rendition and the desire of the lighting application. Light Emitting Diode (LED) lights are fast becoming the choice due to meeting each of these needs. Areas that are not readily visible or accessible to legitimate users may be addressed by motion sensor or dual motion/infra red sensor lights which ignite when motion and the heat register meets the preset measure. These indicate to nearby residents or patrols that the area that they cannot observe has activity occurring and further investigation is warranted.

4. Are parking area entrances/exits limited to the minimum necessary to insure safe travel?

☐ Yes ☐ No ☐ N/A

As previously mentioned, the quick and easy entrance onto the main highway, or several ways to exit the lot, presents the criminal with quick escape routes. Additionally by limiting the number of entrances, the surveillance by the Security Team is improved.

5. Are there signs and/or street numbers that allow for quick locating of the church by emergency services?

☐ Yes ☐ No ☐ N/A

In order to insure quick response to calls for assistance, all churches should be identified with their street address in large numbers over the door or placed according to local ordinance. All churches can insure quick response by identifying their church with appropriate signage as well.

6. Are all non-public access doors, such as the one closest the church secretary or office equipped with a wide-angle viewer, camera or other means of seeing the visitor?

☐ Yes ☐ No ☐ N/A

It is recommended that without some legitimate reason, the church building should be secured during weekdays and when events or services are not being held. All doors through which shipments might be received or visitors to the office might be received should be equipped with a wide angle viewer that allows for a minimum of 160 degree vision. Policies concerning when this door might be accessed and requiring that the user check prior to opening to insure there is no person loitering outside should be part of the overall security procedures for the church.

7. Are fences or other means employed to direct persons to more visible areas?

   ☐ Yes ☐ No ☐ N/A

The strategic placement of fences, planters and other items on a parking lot, entrance way or sidewalk to direct customers, vehicles and pedestrians to a visible location is yet another way that observation opportunities can be enhanced. Any area that is not visible to neighbors or team members should be addressed by some such manner.

8. Is all shrubbery near the building maintained at a height of 3 feet or less?

   ☐ Yes ☐ No ☐ N/A

By maintaining the shrubbery at the recommended three feet or less height, the potential for concealment by criminals and attack of persons leaving the church is greatly reduced. While protecting persons with well trimmed shrubs, the church protects the building as well from burglars.

9. Have trees been trimmed up to a six-foot canopy?

   ☐ Yes ☐ No ☐ N/A

Like the above recommendation, keeping tree canopies trimmed up to six feet provide good visual surveillance opportunity to persons and patrols passing the church, as well as employees and members leaving the church.

10. Are the boundaries clearly defined with signage, fencing, or landscaping?

☐ Yes ☐ No ☐ N/A

Property boundaries should be clearly defined by treatment that demonstrates a transition from one property to another. Low fencing, a change in sidewalk color or texture, fences, and a variety of other means may be employed to accomplish this. It is important that property be defined in order to specify that a different behavior is expected. Private property does not have to tolerate the same behaviors that public property does.

BURGLARY VULNERABILITIES

Criminals committing burglaries are often attracted to churches by the same weaknesses that those committing robberies are, therefore, many of the questions listed will be similar but not always identical. Burglars are often driven by a different reward, if the risks and effort outweigh the reward, the burglar will most likely choose a target elsewhere.

1. Is the church protected by a full or partial see-through fence?

   ☐ Yes ☐ No ☐ N/A

While fencing is not essential, it can provide protection to certain vulnerable areas of the church while closed. If fencing is employed, it is recommended that a minimum 6 foot height chain link or other see-through fencing be used to allow for police patrol surveillance. Typically the use of chain link and fencing designed to restrict access, which is not aesthetically pleasing is limited to problem areas such as the back of a property where it joins a wooded area. Border definition for preventing trespassing and to direct persons to a specific opening may be accomplished by more aesthetically pleasing fencing such as split rail or wrought iron.

2. If fenced, are all potential make shift ladders kept away from the fences?

   ☐ Yes ☐ No ☐ N/A

Fences are designed to restrict access to certain areas and in order to insure their effective use it is imperative that all containers, trees and other items that might assist in climbing the fence be removed.

3. Is concealment next to the building eliminated?

　　□ Yes □ No □ N/A

Reducing the concealment locations around the church reduces the opportunity for burglars to force entry un-detected. Concealment loca-tions can be limited by removal of foliage, large items and/or solid fencing. By removing

concealment the church is open to casual observation.

4. Is the church exterior alarmed?

　　□ Yes □ No □ N/A

Unlike a robbery alarm, the purpose of the burglar alarm is to alert the burglar that he/she has been de-tected and to draw attention to the facility. A combina-tion monitored/audible alarm is ideal to achieve this goal and prevent the burglar from remaining on the scene for a prolonged period. An alarm that is moni-tored off-site only provides less of a prevention aspect than one that sounds audibly and thus is likely to direct attention to the property, which the criminal does not want due to it increasing their potential for detection, observation and capture.

If an alarm is used the church must guard the pass-word and not distribute it widely. All users must be trained in arming and disarming the alarm. The largest cause of false activations is not equipment failure or problems but rather human error.

5. Are all openings to the building secure by some means?

   ☐ Yes ☐ No ☐ N/A

Any ventilation ducts, skylights and windows should be protected with adequate locks. Skylights, vents and any particularly vulnerable windows may need to be reinforced.

6. Are all exterior locks quality deadbolt locks?

   ☐ Yes ☐ No ☐ N/A

All doors should be equipped with commercial grade quality dead bolt locks with a minimum one-inch throw. Any second door  of a double door system should have flush bolts that lock into place at the top and bottom of the non-active door.

7. Are all exterior non-public access doors constructed of solid wood core or metal construction?

   ☐ Yes ☐ No ☐ N/A

The nature of many churches demands glass doors for public access, however other doors that are used by staff or for receiving shipments should be of metal or solid wood core and a minimum of 1 ¾ inch thickness. The strike plate should be reinforced with extra long screws and the door fit snugly in the frame.

The Security Team should conduct a physical inspection of all doors, windows and other portals to ensure that they are properly secured. An improperly functioning lock is not much better than no lock at all.

8. Are all door hinge pins protected from access or removal?

    ☐ Yes ☐ No ☐ N/A

All hinge pins should be non-removable, welded, constructed with an anti-removal stud or located on the inside of the doors.

9. Are there signs visible to the public stating that cash is not retained on the premises?

    ☐ Yes ☐ No ☐ N/A

Signs indicating that, "no cash is stored the premises" should be clearly posted. Such simple techniques as this, indicating the reduced reward to any burglar, goes a long way to their not finding this church an attractive target worth the risk.

10. Are the office doors treated as an exterior door and secured with similar locks?

   ☐ Yes ☐ No ☐ N/A

Typically the office will contain any safe, personal identifying documents of the congregation, computers and other valuables and should be secured using the same criteria of an exterior door. Dependent upon the other items and amount of security desired in the office, one may even consider the installation of an Underwriters Laboratory approved "high security lock."

11. Are all keys controlled and inventoried regularly?

   ☐ Yes ☐ No ☐ N/A

While few should have keys to the church, this seems to be chronic problem. Mechanical keys can easily be copied and become available to disreputable persons. A lock or lock core replacement policy should be instituted that requires the changing of the locks each time a key is compromised, lost or stolen. This becomes very expensive in facilities that all doors are "keyed alike." If an alarm code accompanies the opening process, resetting of the alarm access code may be all that is required.

A best practice regarding mechanical keys (non-electronic) is to key one door differently than others and only issue keys to that door as needed. If the key becomes compromised only one door must be re-keyed. All keys should be controlled by a key log documenting a date of issue and to whom it was issued. An annual physical inspection and inventory of all keys should be implemented.

Electronic access controls utilizing proximity, swipe and other credentialing is the ideal. There are currently wireless electronic control devices on the market that are relatively inexpensive. Using an electronic access control system which includes a method of tracking use and of discontinuing access by computer and absent of the credential would be ideal for the single entrance system described above. The system would pay for its self in a short period of time. Prior to contracting with any business for electronic access controls or security, the church should become familiar with regulations overseeing these companies. Many states regulate the private security field and mandate certain credentials to prove compliance. The most minimal regulations will require registration and background checks of employees of these companies to ensure burglars are not being made privy to the security measures of the client.

12. Are all exterior air conditioning and heat pump units protected from theft?

☐ Yes ☐ No ☐ N/A

In recent years the price of recycled metals more than tripled, creating a new problem of the theft of entire exterior HVAC units. Many churches are vacant during the week and present  an easy theft in the evening. Criminals find it much easier to pull a truck up close to the unit, cut the power with the shut off switch and simple load the entire unit and drive away. To prevent the stripping of air conditioning units of their copper coils, property owners may enclose their unit in a wire cage or padlock their power disconnect box with a quality disc type padlock. This type of lock makes it difficult, if not impossible to cut the lock. Home improvement stores offer many brands of these locks for under $20. There are also commercially available alarm products on the market that monitor the pressure and current to the unit and report any disruptions.

Policies and Procedures

The Team's first task should be the review of any existing Security Policy and Procedures/Crisis Plan. If none exists or is determined to be deficient, the team should begin to develop one or amend the existing ones. This document should define the purpose of the security team, its members, a disclosure statement, role(s) and responsibilities of the Security Team Leader, establish security policies/procedures and crisis plan(s). In that each church has its own set of issues and needs; it is difficult for an outside team to create an effective plan or policies and procedures for the facility. In some cases assistance may be given in developing these plans by local law enforcement agencies, emergency management agencies for the locality and Fire Departments. The below outline should serve to provide a foundation and guide in the development of a plan.

CRISIS PLAN

1. **Title Page**- Name of the church, detailing that the document is the security/crisis plan, include any revision dates.

2. **Table of contents**- Self-explanatory.

3. **Disclosure Statement**- Describe the nature of the document, who it will be disseminated to and that it should be considered a sensitive document and not to be released to the general public.

4. **Security Team**- Give an explanation of the

security team's makeup. If individual names are used, the plan will need to be updated more often. If the use of names, addresses and telephone numbers is desirable, the document may utilize an appendix that lists the team and can easily be changed since it is separate from the body of the plan.

5. **Purpose Statement** - Describes the purpose for the formation of the team and its role in providing security.

6. **Security Team Leader-** Describe the role and responsibilities of the position. The description should also include responsibility. The chain of authority should be clearly established to prevent confusion during a crisis when it is not unusual for members to look to elders, deacons or the minister to lead.

7. **Building/Evacuation Plans** – Self explanatory.

8. **Policy and Procedures section-** This section should include policies that affect the normal everyday security of the facility. Hereafter a sample Building Security Policy is provided.

9. **Crisis Plan Section-** This section should describe how to handle specific crisis situations. It is

recommended that the procedures to handle these situations should be in a simple line-by-line or numbered format for ease of following in a crisis.

Crisis Defined

— A sudden, generally unanticipated event that profoundly and negatively affects a significant segment of the organization and often involves serious injury or death. Includes; Natural situations, man-made situations, accidental situations.

Crisis Management Defined

____ Prior preparation for effectively managing crisis situations by having documented, taught and practiced an organized response to a chaotic event. The response should be designed with priority of protecting life and minimizing injury.

Examples of Items to Be Covered Are:

A. Bomb Threats

Bomb threats are delivered in a several ways. The majority of threats are called in to the target. Sometimes a threat may be communicated in writing. The Alcohol Tobacco and Firearms (A.T.F.) recommends instructing all those that may receive calls, especially those at the telephone switchboard, in what to do if a bomb threat call is received.

A calm response to the caller is essential and may result in obtaining additional information. The bomb threat caller is the best source of information about the bomb. When a bomb threat is called in the A.T.F. advises:

— Keep the caller on the line as long as possible. Ask him/her to repeat the message. Record every word spoken by the person.

— If the caller does not indicate the location of the bomb or the time of possible detonation, ask him/her for this information.

— Inform the caller that the building is occupied and the detonation of a bomb could result in death or serious injury to many innocent people.

— Pay particular attention to background noises, such as motors running, music playing, and any other noise which may give a clue as to the location of the caller.

— Listen closely to the voice (male, female), voice quality (calm, excited), accents, and speech impediments. Immediately after the caller hangs up, report the threat to the person designated by management to receive such information .

— Report the information immediately to the police department, fire department, A.T.F., F.B.I., and other appropriate agencies. The sequence of notification should be established in the bomb incident plan.

— Remain available, as law enforcement personnel will want to interview you.

When a written threat is received, save all materials, including any envelope or container. Once the message is recognized as a bomb threat, further unnecessary handling should be avoided. Every possible effort must be made to retain evidence such as fingerprints, handwriting or typewriting, paper, and postal marks. These will prove essential in tracing the threat and identifying the writer.

Bomb Threat Checklists which aid in a call taker gathering information are available on the Homeland Security Website, from FEMA, A.T.F. and many other similar agencies.

— Suspicious Packages

- For example a procedure for handling such packages might state, If a letter or parcel is received that is considered suspicious, the church staff should be directed as to what action to take. Bomb threats, suspicious mail and suggested handling is described in documents available from the F.B.I., the A.T.F. and the Postal Inspection.

- An evacuation plan must also be developed. Those involved in any evacuation should be trained in how to evacuate the building during a bomb threat or other threat. Priority of evacuation should be considered in the plan. Typically the plans specify that the priority is to evacuate the floor levels above and below the danger area in order to remove those persons from danger first. The local police and fire departments should be asked to assist in considerations. This will avoid the possibility of conflicting policies of who decides when to evacuate etc.

B. Armed Attacker

The possibility of an armed attacker is a very real scenario that all houses of worship should address.

- Plans should ensure that someone notify police and provide as much information as possible. It is better to have too many calls rather there be a possibility that nobody calls.

- Plans should specify the Security Team actions such as:

  — Evacuating the area

  — Evaluating the perpetrator

  — Isolate the attacker

  — Negotiation

  — Remaining calm

  — Avoiding heroics

  — Keeping a safe, non-intimidating distance

  — Avoiding abrupt sporadic movements

  — Looking for cover to quickly get to if necessary

C. Abduction or missing child

If the church operates a daycare or other child directed services, the team should consider this in planning.

D. Hostage Situations

Due to the high probability of domestic issues finding their way to the church building, and the high percentage of hostage situations being domestic relationship related, it is essential that this potential be addressed.

Hostage situations are extremely dangerous and difficult to plan for due to the variance from one situation to the next. A plan may include some of the following information and duties of the team, but certainly would not be limited to these items.

Identification of Charge or designated individual will assume charge of the situation until the arrival of the Police Department at the scene. The Security Team should work closely with the designee to ensure that this plan of action is safely achieved.

Containment: Appropriate actions should be taken to *isolate the hostage taker and the victims* under his control. It is important that no others be exposed to the hostage taker.

Evacuation: Immediately evacuate the building and ensure that egress is done in a manner that insures those leaving do not go near the area controlled by the hostage taker.

Re-entry: Ensure that no individuals enter or re-enter the building.

Contact 911: Immediately have someone contact 911 and give all available information to the dispatcher who will relay the information to the Police Department. Ensure that the caller remains on the line with the 911 dispatcher until police actually arrive at the scene. This will ensure that accurate, detailed information in relayed to responding officers and church leaders can respond to requests of the police department.

Local Law Enforcement: Upon response of law enforcement, control of the scene will be assumed by that Department. *It is important that the items such as building keys and detailed building plans be made available to the police department, preferably in advance.* Important information such as camera and monitoring locations, hearing and broadcast devices, motion sensors, location of radios, availability of phones, *et cetera*, be conveyed to the police department. Anecdotal information regarding the cause of the incident, identity of the hostages and hostage takers, and their location in the building is of great importance. Someone who is knowledgeable of the building design needs to describe the premises using the detailed building plans.

Negotiations: It is important to remember that it is usually the philosophy of law enforcement to end a hostage situation through negotiating tactics. Often it is a lengthy process. An assault by law enforcement is only used when all indications are that the hostage taker will harm the hostages and that lives will in fact be saved through such an assault.

E. Handling of Threats

The potential for a directed attack against a church leader is significant. It is recommended that you remove the photographs of leaders from any web site and signage marking the reserved parking for significant leaders be limited from identifying who parks in which areas.

- A policy directing the reporting of all threats against individuals or the church should be implemented. All threats should be reported to the police but also to the security team. The policy should direct how this will be done and may direct any other actions to be taken. The procedure should address team actions if a person who has communicated a threat is observed at, or near the church. At a minimum the procedure may require the police to be called, someone with mobile communications to maintain observation from a safe distance, and the securing of all buildings to prevent entry. If the threat is written, procedures should dictate reporting but also handling of the letter/note. Handle the message as little as possible in order to pre-serve any evidence.

F. Special Events

The church should have operational plans or guide-lines for addressing special large events. A sample of a church huge event plan that may be used as guid-ance in developing event plans is provided below.

PRIOR TO EVENTS

For all events, consider :

- ❏ anticipated crowd size,
- ❏ advance publicity,
- ❏ date predictability,
- ❏ presence of High Profile Speakers, (Potential Tar-gets)
- ❏ symbolism of Event, (Which might attract anti-event persons i.e. Gospel Meeting with pro-life theme)
- ❏ Impact of a bombing, killing or other critical inci-dent.

Determine if a security presence is necessary.

Determine the scope of security presence required by writing an "Event Security Plan" to share with the team.

Determine who is to be notified concerning unusual or special security precautions, arrangements, purchases, etc. Create a schedule of contract security officers if needed. (If used) Obtain approval for expenditure from leadership.

> **If contract security is used efforts should be taken to select, train and use one company for all such events. Be sure to check that all employee guards have had a background check completed and that no felons, sexual offenders, etc. are assigned.

Provide security officers with layout of property and buildings. They should tour the facilities each time before starting an event, noting entrances and exits, and the locations where people will gather (i.e. auditorium, etc.) Security officers should be trained on church policies and expectations concerning their duties, emergencies, and the handling of disorderly persons and those who may attempt to commit criminal acts.

Officers assigned to traffic control duties should not be considered primary security officers. Their attention and focus will be on traffic, not security.

Notify all required persons of the Security Plan details and ask for equipment checks on 2-way radios, emergency lighting and any other equipment involved in the Plan to ensure proper functioning.

Check parking requirements for Event. Parking may or may not be included in the Security Team Leader responsibilities but parking must be addressed due to potential conflict arising from such issues and due to the necessity of access by emergency responders.

Notify the local Police Department of the event and provide them a copy of the plan, contacts and identifying the nature of the event, threats considered or received, and any actions requested of them, such as assigned area patrol, pre-event sweep by bomb dogs, parking enforcement during critical hours, on-site meeting with Security Force during event. The Police Department may charge a fee and expenditures must be approved by the authorized leadership.

Draft notice concerning special traffic, parking or other arrangements that will affect neighbors. Always draft notice as a neighborly notification, expressing commitment to safety and welfare of entire neighborhood. If security is a primary concern, say so, but if not, tell neighbors the notice is out of concern for traffic or parking considerations only. Do not be an alarmist. Ask for neighbor awareness of unusual or suspicious persons or events and ask them to call the police or call Security Coordinator (give cell phone number) to report such things. Most event notices can be mailed to neighbors.

THE EVENT

All officers should be introduced to each other before an event and post or assignment names, numbers or codes should be shared with all to facilitate communication.

Events that have enhanced or significant risk of attracting violence may require the presence of a trained compensated off-duty plainclothes officer or security team member at each entrance to monitor people arriving.

Duties will include:

- observing appearance for bulges or other signs of weapons,
- checking any large bag or container,
- requiring that backpacks and similar containers be left at the front door (after inspection) whenever they would take up too much space at a large event,
- greeting and interviewing suspicious persons, and
- making judgments about denying access for good reason.

Any person assigned this task needs to be qualified to deal courteously, respectfully and tactfully with people. This person will be dealing, in most cases, with members.

A Supervisor of any event and the Security Force needs to be familiar with evacuation and/or secure-in-place procedures established. This includes a plain-clothes officer or team member monitoring people entering an event.

The Security Coordinator or Supervisor needs to know who will be present to represent the church to the media in the event that an arrest occurs or other policy decisions are required – i.e. Elder, Minister or other.

G. Negative media coverage in response to church sermon, discipline, doctrine or event.

- Although one might not consider the media coverage as a specific crisis for the church it might be. Remember our definition of crisis was a sudden, generally unanticipated event that profoundly and negatively affects a significant segment of the church. Now consider the harm that a negative media account can have on the church. Perhaps a child molester was arrested and had just attended the church two days ago for the first time but the media discovers that he attends the church. Which makes a better headline church member arrested for child molestation or man arrested for child molestation? Suppose the Minister preaches a sermon on marriage and indicates through scripture that the Bible is clear that marriage is between a man and a woman. If that sermon was heard on a radio program or otherwise learned of during the same day news came out about a change in same-sex marriage laws, it might make a good link for the media. We cannot refuse to speak the truth for fear of negative publicity but we do need to be prepared to address the media when such situations arise and to provide the best and most honest answer possible. We need to be prepared so that we are not tricked or misunderstood. Below are some guidelines that should be studied by whoever is designated to answer media inquiries for the church.

Guidelines for Communicating with the Media in Times of Crisis

1. The primary goal should be to keep the public, specifically the brethren, informed about the crisis honestly while trying to maintain the privacy of those involved.

2. As soon as possible, prepare a <u>written statement</u> that gives the basic facts clearly and concisely. Two or three minutes spent writing down some specific points is valuable. If there is time, try to anticipate what some of the questions will be and prepare answers. In the past when I served in my law enforcement agency to answer media inquires, I found writing down the points I wanted covered (positive points) and giving it to the television reporter a few minutes prior served me well. In most cases, because my written information was the last things they saw, the questions were related to those things. News people will always want to know: who, what, when, where, why, and how. Use the same facts in dealing with all media so the story is consistent and no appearance of favoritism is indicated.

3. Don't presume to tell a reporter what is or isn't news-worthy. Never — **absolutely never** — tell anything misleading to a reporter. While we would not assume any in the church would lie, some larger churches employ media representatives who may not be guided by the same moral guidelines. Tell the bad news quickly; get it over with. It may be your only chance to set the record straight. If the media think you're hiding some-thing, they're likely to dig hard for information from other sources and sensationalize the story, in some

cases they may even "create" the story. Without facts they will most certainly report events less accurately. Protecting and enhancing the church's credibility is important.

4. If you don't understand the question, say so. Repeating the reporter's question may pose a danger because the tape can be edited to sound like you agree whether you do or not. Suppose the reporter asks, "How are you handling this attack on your faith?" Don't respond, "We are handling this attack on our faith by . . ." Instead, respond in your own words to the effect that, "The church is strong and had in place plans to address any situation." Always try to answer with the positive actions of the church in conjunction with describing the event.

5. Answer each question and then be silent! *"In the multitude of words there wanteth not sin: but he that refraineth his lips is wise." (Proverbs 10:19)* Stick with your statement.

Don't embellish it and don't respond to media pressure to chat about it. Don't think because the microphone is lowered that it is off. Do not say more "off-record" than you would on-record. Don't let a reporter's friendly, sympathetic manner disarm you into giving him/her additional information. Don't assume any chatty comments "are off the record" even if you say they are.

6. Remember that conflict is news, and reporters often frame their questions to bring out the conflict or emotion in a story. Reporters often attempt to link a local story to a national debate or topic. A person disrupting the church service due to the preacher adhering strictly to the biblical definition of marriage resulting in the disruptive person's arrest may turn into a larger debate on gay marriage. One must be prepared for that possibility. If the church speaks to the disruption, stick to the act, the disruption and do not speculate or address the mind-set of the individual.

7. If a reporter asks several questions at once, say something like, "You've asked me several questions here. . . where would you like me to begin?" If a reporter interrupts you before you've finished answered your question, pause, let the reporter finish, and then continue your answer. Don't let the reporter get you off track or tell you when you've finished your answer. However, don't go into lengthy detail or run off with the interview either.

8. Reporters are under constant deadlines, but no deadline is so important that it's worth making an inaccurate

statement. If a reporter says he/she has deadline problems, ask how long you have to get the information, and then try to obtain it within that amount of time.

9. It is best not to answer a query with "No comment." Otherwise, the reporters may report you wouldn't answer questions or may interpret for themselves why you aren't answering. Instead, say, "I can't share that information with you right now, but I will call you as soon as I can release it." (And do call them). Or say, "I don't know the answer, but I should have it in an hour (two hours or whatever is accurate). Please call me." If you can't reveal information at all, tell the reporters why. Examples: Relatives of an injured person haven't been notified yet or revealing the identity of a witness would jeopardize an investigation, etc.

10. After you provide the written statement to the media or answer subsequent questions, keep a media log of whom you speak to and what you give them, whether it is the basic statement or a subsequent update. This allows you to track which media received what information.

SECURING THE FAITHFUL

Checklist of Tips for Working with the Media[7]

Don't

- ✓ DON'T try to keep the media out.
- ✓ DON'T say "no comment." Otherwise, the reporters may report you wouldn't answer questions or may interpret for themselves why you aren't answering.
- ✓ DON'T ad-lib.
- ✓ DON'T speak "off the record."
- ✓ DON'T speculate.
- ✓ DON'T try to cover-up or blame anyone for anything.
- ✓ DON'T repeat negative/misleading words.
- ✓ DON'T play favorites among media.

Do

- ✓ Emphasize your good record.
- ✓ Be accurate and cooperate as best you can.
- ✓ Be prepared for and prepare in advance a response to questions which might violate confidentiality or hinder the police investigation.

---

7 Atkinson, Anne PhD. Policy Works Ltd. For Virginia Department of Education. 2002. *Resource Guide for Crisis Management in Virginia Schools.*
Code of Tennessee
Code of Kentucky
Code of Texas

✓ Insist that reporters respect the privacy rights of your members.

✓ Speak to reporters in plain English.

✓ When asked a question and you don't know the answer, say so, then offer to find out and call the reporter back.

H. **Other Crisis** including; natural disaster, death of a church leader, teacher and any other crisis event.

Building Security Policy

A short version of a Security Policy that even the smallest congregation should have at a minimum is provided below. The policy does not address crisis issues but is more of a day to day policy for regular services.

Church Building Security Policy

The following conditions have been established by the church pertaining to security of the church services for attendees before, during and after services. Churches represent a unique challenge to protect due their open and inviting nature. Protecting a church requires a balanced approach and the leadership of the church have implemented the following policies and procedures to mitigate risk without interfering with the mission of outreach and leading the lost to Christ.

1. During time when only the Minister may be present on the property, he will enter through the door nearest his office and once inside secure that door. He should be able to detect visitors by _____ (explain)_____. Additionally, appointments may be made by calling the office to arrange a mutually convenient time to meet.

Securing the Faithful

a. The Minister shall endeavor to avoid all appearances of impropriety. As such, he will never counsel a member of the opposite sex or child alone. When counseling a woman, he will have another woman present or at least within view of an open office door. He may counsel a woman with another man present if a woman is not available.

b. The Minister shall make the leadership of the church leadership or Security Teas Leader aware of any domestic violence potential situations or threats within the congregation of which he is aware.

c. In that the Minister may offend certain groups through proclaiming the truth, he may receive personal threats and shall also make the leadership aware of any such threats to his person, his family or the congregation, no matter how veiled they may be.

d. If the Minister receives an after-hours call by a member or attendee with a request to meet at the building, their home or in any private environment caution will be taken. The Minister will contact an Elder, Deacon or Security Team Member to meet and accompany him to the building or location and will advise the caller that he must find someone to come with him and then call them back. The Minister will also attempt to identify the nature of the emergency in advance. If there are no persons available to assist the Minister may agree to meet in a public venue such as a restaurant.

2. A security team of at least _____ men will be created and responsible for certain duties. One person will be designated as "Team leader" and be responsible for facility security. Prior to services all doors except the auditorium main entrance doors will be locked. A single doors to lower level classrooms may be unlocked prior to class time but after classes are scheduled to begin a members (Which will be assigned) will lock all lower lever doors from ingress but not from egress.) The assigned individual may assist any late arrivals in entrance, otherwise classroom teachers will monitor any entry near their classrooms and offer to assist any persons not known to the congregation by speaking to them through the locked door and referring the stranger to main entrance or may otherwise handle as instructed by the security team leader..

3. Once the Worship service has begun, one of the Se-

curity Team Members assigned to do so will secure all doors except for the _____ list_____ and will close the doors to the auditorium. This individual will be responsible for greeting any late arrivals in the vestibule and will be trained in evaluating indicators of nervousness, and potential violence. Once the visitor enters the member will follow and take a seat behind the individual, if they are unfamiliar with them or detect any indications of suspicious behavior, being prepared to take physical actions, as authorized, if needed to prevent harm.

4. Signs noting reserved parking may be erected but no signs will be erected stating whom the parking is reserved for either by name or by position. This will be done to protect targeting individuals in leadership positions of the congregation.

5. No firearms will be permitted within the building by any persons other than law enforcement, unless granted exception by congregational leadership in advance for the protection of the congregants. Exceptions will only be granted if the leadership can determine that the members is proficient in use and approved to carry such weapon concealed and the security team is made aware of the individual that will be carrying con-

cealed. Signs may be posted to indicate that persons with weapons should secure the weapons in locked compartments within their vehicle and which includes a notice that the church has taken measures to protect attendees. An example of the sign may read, "We recognize the rights of individuals to carry firearms however the church allows only persons authorized by leadership which have been trained in security policies to carry firearms in the church. We ask that you secure your firearms in locked compartments within your vehicle to enhance security operations within the church." No member will carry a firearm in open view.

6. In the event a bomb threat is received, law enforcement will be notified and the facility will be evacuated 15 minutes prior to the expected time of any detonation. The evacuation will remain in effect until 15 min after the stated detonation time, the all clear is given by local authorities or the necessity to extend it is determined. If the threat is received during bible class, each teacher will quickly look around their classroom for anything "out of place" or that does not belong. They will not touch the item but report it to the security team after getting the students to safety. All present will evacuate via the closest doors and into the Fill in this area with the appropriate response . Teachers will

be responsible for accounting for their class.

7. In the event of a crisis of any kind all media inquiries to the church will be directed to <u>list the individual here.</u>

8. A set number of keys _____#_____ shall be made to the ___DESIGNATED_____ doors. These keys shall be the only keys issued those using the fellowship hall. Any use of the auditorium will require a member to be present to open and close the facility. Only __#____keys will be made to the auditorium level doors. Only _____keys shall be issued the _____(list any other doors)_____ door closest to _____.

9. The security team will receive all keys initially and as-sign them as directed by leadership. The Team shall maintain a key log which identifies which key is assigned out and to whom. All keys will be audited annually to insure their physical existence and loca-tion.

10. If a key is lost, a concern due to an unaccounted for key or other appropriate cause, church leadership may direct any or all doors be re-keyed or the locks replaced.

11. The security team will periodically inspect the pre-mises and report any security issues to the leadership for action to include; inoperative exterior lighting, ap-

parent attempts at entry (prying, broken glass etc.), vandalism, policy change needs and concerns.

Concluding Comments

In the world of security the idea of addressing safety is considered under the term of "risk." Experts state that risk can be addressed in several ways. First the risk(s) may be avoided. In the church environment this would mean simply closing the doors and serving only those known to us. This is not possible in the church, if we are to obey the command to "go." The remaining areas addressing risk are possible to a degree. They are; risk reduction, risk spreading, risk transfer and risk acceptance.

The church may reduce risk as pertaining to financial losses by regular deposits, for example. Risk spreading involves taking steps to delay the criminal, detect them and so on. These are discussed in detail in this text. There comes a time when even our best laid plans may fail and the church may suffer some loss. The loss (or risk) is transferred through the church having insurance. Finally the church has to decide that certain risks are acceptable. Obviously we are not referring to injuries or death but the church leadership will have to weigh the cost, the trouble and the effect on the outreach efforts in implementing safety measures. If the cost in these cases outweighs the risk, it may be that the risk simply has to be accepted. In any event the leadership of the church must make some very difficult decisions in mitigating the vulnerabilities to the church and minimizing the consequences of any attack.

While this material is only a beginning in the planning for the church, I hope that it will at the very least start the conversation on how we may Secure the Faithful. May God bless his church and those who serve him faithfully!

> *That the saying might be fulfilled, which he spake, Of them which thou gavest me have I lost none.* (John 18:9)

Appendix 1

Laws Relevant to Religious Institutions in Virginia

These laws were current as of January 2014. Verification of the accuracy is advised as laws frequently change.

Some of the content not pertaining specifically to churches and faith organizations or members is not included but the sections may be listed intentionally without content.

§ 18.2-57. Assault and battery.

A. Any person who commits a simple assault or assault and battery is guilty of a Class 1 misdemeanor, and if the person intentionally selects the person against whom a simple assault is committed because of his race, religious conviction, color or national origin, the penalty upon conviction shall include a term of confinement of at least six months, 30 days of which shall be a mandatory minimum term of confinement.

B. However, if a person intentionally selects the person against whom an assault and battery resulting in bodily injury is committed because of his race, religious conviction, color or national origin, the person is guilty of a Class 6 felony, and the penalty upon conviction shall include a term of confinement of at least six months, 30 days of which shall be a mandatory minimum term of confinement.

C. In addition, …

§ 18.2-75. Conscience clause.

Nothing in §§ 18.2-72, 18.2-73 or § 18.2-74 shall require a hospital or other medical facility or physician to admit any patient under the provisions hereof for the purpose of performing an abortion. In addition, any person who shall state in writing an objection to any abortion or all abortions on personal, ethical, moral or religious grounds shall not be required to participate in procedures which will result in such abortion, and the refusal of such person, hospital or other medical facility to participate therein shall not form the basis of any claim for damages on account of such refusal or for any disciplinary or recriminatory action against such person, nor shall any such person be denied employment because of such objection or refusal. The written objection shall remain in effect until such person shall revoke it in writing or terminate his association with the facility with which it is filed.

§ 18.2-121. Entering property of another for purpose of damaging it, etc.

It shall be unlawful for any person to enter the land, dwelling, outhouse or any other building of another for the purpose of damaging such property or any of the contents thereof or in any manner to interfere with the rights of the owner, user or the occupant thereof to use such property free from interference.

Any person violating the provisions of this section shall be guilty of a Class 1 misdemeanor. However, if a person intentionally selects the property entered because of the race, religious conviction, color or national origin of the owner, user or occupant of the property, the person shall be guilty of a Class 6 felony, and the penalty upon conviction shall include a term of confinement of at least six months, 30 days of which shall be a mandatory minimum term of confinement.

§ 18.2-280. Willfully discharging firearms in public places.

A. If any person willfully discharges or causes to be discharged any firearm in any street in a city or town, or in any place of public business or place of public gathering, and such conduct results in bodily injury to another person, he shall be guilty of a Class 6 felony. If such conduct does not result in bodily injury to another person, he shall be guilty of a Class 1 misdemeanor.

B. If any person willfully discharges or causes to be discharged any firearm upon the buildings and grounds of any public, private or religious elementary, middle or high school, he shall be guilty of a Class 4 felony, unless he is engaged in a program or curriculum sponsored by or conducted with permission of a public, private or religious school.

C. If any person willfully discharges or causes to be discharged any firearm upon any public property within 1,000 feet of the property line of any public, private or religious elementary, middle or high school property he shall be guilty of a Class 4 felony, unless he is engaged in lawful hunting.

D. This section shall not apply to any law-enforcement officer in the performance of his official duties nor to any other person whose said willful act is otherwise justifiable or excusable at law in the protection of his life or property, or is otherwise specifically authorized by law.

E. Nothing in this statute shall preclude the Commonwealth from electing to prosecute under any other applicable provision of law instead of this section.

§ 18.2-283. Carrying dangerous weapon to place of religious worship.

If any person carry any gun, pistol, bowie knife, dagger or other dangerous weapon, without good and sufficient reason, to a place of worship while a meeting for religious purposes is being held at such place he shall be guilty of a Class 4 misdemeanor.

§ 18.2-415. Disorderly conduct in public places.

A person is guilty of disorderly conduct if, with the intent to cause public inconvenience, annoyance or alarm, or recklessly creating a risk thereof, he:

A. ...

B. Willfully or being intoxicated, whether willfully or not, and whether such intoxication results from self-administered alcohol or other drug of whatever nature, disrupts any funeral, memorial service, or meeting of the governing body of any political subdivision of this Commonwealth or a division or agency thereof, or of any school, literary society or place of religious worship, if the disruption (i) prevents or interferes with the orderly conduct of the funeral, memorial service, or meeting or (ii) has a direct tendency to cause acts of violence by the person or persons at whom, individually, the disruption is directed; or

C. ...

However, the conduct prohibited under subdivision A, B or C of this section shall not be deemed to include the utterance or display of any words or to include conduct otherwise made punishable under this title. The person in charge of any such building, place, conveyance, meeting, operation or activity may eject therefrom any person who violates any provision of this section, with the aid, if necessary, of any persons who may be called upon for such purpose.

The governing bodies of counties, cities and towns are authorized to adopt ordinances prohibiting and punishing the acts and conduct prohibited by this section, provided that the punishment fixed therefor shall not exceed that prescribed for a Class 1 misdemeanor. A person violating any provision of this section shall be guilty of a Class 1 misdemeanor.

§ 18.2-423.1. Placing swastika on certain property with intent to intimidate; penalty; prima facie evidence of intent.

It shall be unlawful for any person or persons, with the intent of intimidating another person or group of persons, to place or cause to be placed a swastika on any church, synagogue or other building or place used for religious worship, or on any school, educational facility or community center owned or operated by a church or religious body.

A violation of this section shall be punishable as a Class 6 felony.

§ 18.2-423. Burning cross on property of another or public place with intent to intimidate; penalty; prima facie evidence of intent.

It shall be unlawful for any person or persons, with the intent of intimidating any person or group of persons, to burn, or cause to be burned, a cross on the property of another, a highway or other public place. Any person who shall violate any provision of this section shall be guilty of a Class 6 felony.

Any such burning of a cross shall be prima facie evidence of an intent to intimidate a person or group of persons.

§ 18.2-423.01. Burning object on property of another or a highway or other public place with intent to intimidate; penalty.

A. Any person who, with the intent of intimidating any person or group of persons, burns an object on the private property of another without permission, is guilty of a Class 6 felony.

B. Any person who, with the intent of intimidating any person or group of persons, burns an object on a highway or other public place in a manner having a direct tendency to place another person in reasonable fear or apprehension of death or bodily injury is guilty of a Class 6 felony

§ 18.2-79. Burning or destroying meeting house, etc.

If any person maliciously burns, or by the use of any explosive device or substance, maliciously destroys, in whole or in part, or causes to be burned or destroyed, or aids, counsels, or procures the burning or destroying, of any meeting house, courthouse, townhouse, college, academy, schoolhouse, or other building erected for public use except an asylum, hotel, jail, prison or church or building owned or leased by a church that is immediately adjacent to a church, or any banking house, warehouse, storehouse, manufactory, mill, or other house, whether the property of himself or of another person, not usually occupied by persons lodging therein at night, at a time when any person is therein, or if he maliciously sets fire to anything, or causes to be set on fire, or aids, counsels, or procures the setting on fire of anything, by the burning whereof any building mentioned in this section is burned, at a time when any person is therein, he shall be guilty of a Class 3 felony. If such offense is committed when no person is in such building mentioned in this section, the offender shall be guilty of a Class 4 felony.

§ 18.2-85. Manufacture, possession, use, etc., of fire bombs or explosive materials or devices; penalties.

… Any person who (i) possesses materials with which fire bombs or explosive materials or devices can be made with the intent to manufacture fire bombs or explosive materials or devices or, (ii) manufactures, transports, distributes, possesses or uses a fire bomb or explosive materials or devices shall be guilty of a Class 5 felony. Any person who constructs, uses, places, sends, or causes to be sent any hoax explosive device so as to intentionally cause another person to believe that such device is a bomb or explosive shall be guilty of a Class 6 felony.

Nothing in this section shall prohibit the authorized manufacture, transportation, distribution, use or possession of any material, substance, or device by a member of the armed forces of the United States, fire fighters or law-enforcement officers, nor shall it prohibit the manufacture, transportation, distribution, use or possession of any material, substance or device to be used solely for scientific research, educational purposes or for any lawful purpose, subject to the provisions of §§ 27-97 and 27-97.2.

§ 18.2-308.01. Carrying a concealed handgun with a permit.

A. The prohibition against carrying a concealed handgun in clause (i) of subsection A of § 18.2-308 shall not apply to a person who has a valid concealed handgun permit issued pursuant to this article. The person issued the permit shall have such permit on his person at all times during which he is carrying a concealed handgun and shall display the permit and a photo identification issued by a government agency of the Commonwealth or by the U.S. Department of Defense or U.S. State Department (passport) upon demand by a law-enforcement officer. A person to whom a nonresident permit is issued shall have such permit on his person at all times when he is carrying a concealed handgun in the Commonwealth and shall display the permit on demand by a law-enforcement officer. A person whose permit is extended due to deployment shall carry with him and display, upon request of a law-enforcement officer, a copy of the documents required by subsection B of § 18.2-308.010.

B. Failure to display the permit and a photo identification upon demand by a law-enforcement officer shall be punishable by a $25 civil penalty, which shall be paid into the state treasury. Any attorney for the Commonwealth of the county or city in which the alleged violation occurred may bring an action to recover the civil penalty. A court may waive such penalty upon presentation to the court of a valid permit and a government-issued photo identification. Any law-enforcement officer may issue a summons for the civil violation of failure to display the concealed handgun permit and photo identification upon demand.

C. The granting of a concealed handgun permit pursuant to this article shall not thereby authorize the possession of any handgun or other weapon on property or in places where such possession is otherwise prohibited by law or is prohibited by the owner of private property.

§ 18.2-128. Trespass upon church or school property.

A. Any person who, without the consent of some person authorized to give such consent, goes or enters upon, in the nighttime, the premises or property of any church or upon any school property for any purpose other than to attend a meeting or service held or conducted in such church or school property, shall be guilty of a Class 3 misdemeanor.

B. It shall be unlawful for any person, whether or not a church member or student, to enter upon or remain upon any church or school property in violation of (i) any direction to vacate the property by a person authorized to give such direction or (ii) any posted notice which contains such information, posted at a place where it reasonably may be seen. Each time such person enters upon or remains on the posted premises or after such direction that person refuses to vacate such property, it shall constitute a separate offense.

A violation of this subsection shall be punishable as a Class 1 misdemeanor, except that any person, other than a parent, who violates this subsection on school property with the intent to abduct a student shall be guilty of a Class 6 felony.

C. For purposes of this section: (i) "school property" includes a school bus as defined in § 46.2-100 and (ii) "church" means any place of worship and includes any educational building or community center owned or leased by a church.

§ 18.2-127. Injuries to churches, church property, cemeteries, burial grounds, etc.; penalty.

A. Any person who willfully or maliciously commits any of the following acts is guilty of a Class 1 misdemeanor:

1. Destroys, removes, cuts, breaks, or injures any tree, shrub, or plant on any church property or within any cemetery or lot of any memorial or monumental association;

2. Destroys, mutilates, injures, or removes and carries away any flowers, wreaths, vases, or other ornaments placed within any church or on church property, or placed upon or around any grave, tomb, monument, or lot in any cemetery, graveyard, or other place of burial; or

3. Obstructs proper ingress to and egress from any church or any cemetery or lot belonging to any memorial or monumental association.

B. Any person who willfully or maliciously destroys, mutilates, defaces, injures, or removes any object or structure permanently attached or affixed within any church or on church property, any tomb, monument, gravestone, or other structure placed within any cemetery, graveyard, or place of burial, or within any lot belonging to any memorial or monumental association, or any fence, railing, or other work for the protection or ornament of any tomb, monument, gravestone, or other structure aforesaid, or of any cemetery lot within any cemetery is guilty of a Class 6 felony. A person convicted under this section who is required to pay restitution by the court shall be required to pay restitution to the church, if the property damaged is property of the church, or to the owner of a cemetery, if the property damaged is located within such cemetery regardless of whether the property damaged is owned by the cemetery or by another person.

C. This section shall not apply to any work which is done by the authorities of a church or congregation in the maintenance or improvement of any church property or any burial ground or cemetery belonging to it and under its management or control and which does not injure or result in the removal of a tomb, monument, gravestone, grave marker or vault. For purposes of this section, "church" shall mean any place of worship, and "church property" shall mean any educational building or community center owned or rented by a church.

CIVIL ACTION CODE

§ 8.01-42.1. Civil action for racial, religious, or ethnic harassment, violence or vandalism.

A. An action for injunctive relief or civil damages, or both, shall lie for any person who is subjected to acts of (i) intimidation or harassment or (ii) violence directed against his person; or (iii) vandalism directed against his real or personal property, where such acts are motivated by racial, religious, or ethnic animosity.

B. Any aggrieved party who initiates and prevails in an action authorized by this section shall be entitled to damages, including punitive damages, and in the discretion of the court to an award of the cost of the litigation and reasonable attorneys' fees in an amount to be fixed by the court.

C. The provisions of this section shall not apply to any actions between an employee and his employer, or between or among employees of the same employer, for damages arising out of incidents occurring in the workplace or arising out of the employee-employer relationship.

Appendix 2

Laws Relevant to Religious Institutions in Tennessee

Some of these laws were paraphrased or notes added as to the content rather than listing the law.

Verification of the accuracy is advised as laws frequently change. Some of the content not pertaining specifically to churches and faith organizations or members is not included but the sections may be listed intentionally without content.

State Constitution

Article I, Section 26

That the citizens of this State have a right to keep and to bear arms for their common defense; but the Legislature shall have power, by law, to regulate the wearing of arms with a view to prevent crime.

Open Car Carry

Firearms may be openly carried in cars **only** with a permit/license.

Places Off-Limits (Note churches are not listed)

In any room where a judicial proceeding is taking place (39-17-1306)

Schools (39-17-1309 and 39-17-1310)

Some local public Parks and recreational property (39-17-1311)

Any Penal Institution (39-16-201)

Any place with a properly posted sign per (39-17-1359)

Opinion of the Attorney General of Tennessee

Re: Prohibiting firearms on private property

April 9, 2007

Opinion No. 07-43

Owners of private property may prohibit the possession of handguns and other weapons on their property. To be effective, the owner must post a written notice that satisfies the requirements of Tenn. Code Ann. § 39-17-1359(a), which states, in pertinent part:

The notice shall be in English but a notice may also be posted in any language used by patrons, customers or persons who frequent the place where weapon possession is prohibited. In addition to the sign, notice may also include the international circle and slash symbolizing the prohibition of the item within the circle. The sign shall be of a size that is plainly visible to the average person entering the building, premises or property and shall contain language substantially similar to the following:

PURSUANT TO § 39-17-1359, THE OWNER/OPERATOR OF THIS PROPERTY HAS BANNED WEAPONS ON THIS PROPERTY, OR WITHIN THIS BUILDING OR THIS PORTION OF THIS BUILDING. FAILURE TO COMPLY WITH THIS PROHIBITION IS PUNISHABLE AS A CRIMINAL ACT UNDER STATE LAW AND MAY SUBJECT THE VIOLATOR TO A FINE OF NOT MORE THAN FIVE HUNDRED DOLLARS ($500).

Tenn. Code Ann. § 39-17-1359(a) also prescribes the requirement for the posting of notices. It states, in the relevant part:

Posted notices shall be displayed in prominent locations, including all entrances primarily used by persons entering the building, portion of the building or buildings where weapon possession is prohibited. If the possession of weapons is also prohibited on the premises of the property as well as within the confines of a building located on the property, the notice shall be posted at all entrances to the premises that are primarily used by persons entering the property.

Tenn. Code Ann. § 39-17-1359(a).

46-1-313. Trespass on or injury to cemetery property -- Interference with processions or religious exercises -- Penalty.

(a) No person shall willfully destroy, deface, or injure any monument, tomb, gravestone, or other structure placed in the cemetery, or any roadway, walk, fence or enclosure in or around the cemetery, or injure any tree, plant or shrub, or hunt or shoot, play at any game or amusement, or loiter for lascivious or lewd purposes in the cemetery, or interfere, by words or actions, with any funeral procession or any religious exercises.

(b) (1) A violation of this section is a Class E felony.

(2) Following conviction of a person for violating subsection (a), evidence of damages sustained as a result of the violation shall be presented to the jury, which shall ascertain the total amount of the damages. The court shall then render judgment in that amount against the offender in favor of the cemetery and/or the other aggrieved parties and shall order the offender to make full restitution for the damages. Execution of the judgment shall issue as in other civil cases. The order of restitution shall be in addition to other sanctions imposed pursuant to subdivision (b)(1).

Human Rights- Employment Related Discrimination

4-21-405. Religious groups exempted.

This chapter shall not apply to religious corporations, associations, educational institutions, or societies, with respect to the employment of individuals of a particular religion to perform work connected with the carrying on by the corporation, association, educational institution, or society, of its religious activities.

Terrorism Prevention and Response Act of 2002

39-13-809. Religious justification for violence or criminal activity prohibited.

Religious justification for violence or criminal activity prohibited by this part shall not be considered a justification or a defense pursuant to chapter 11, part 6 of this title, nor shall it prohibit prosecution pursuant to this part.

49-4-934. HOPE scholarship -- Dependent child of full-time religious worker.

(a) Notwithstanding any provision of this part to the contrary, a student who is a Tennessee citizen and a dependent child of a full-time religious worker shall be eligible for a Tennessee HOPE scholarship as an entering freshman if the student meets all eligibility requirements for the scholarship, except that, while the parent is serving in another nation as a religious worker, the student does not reside in Tennessee immediately preceding the date of application for financial assistance and the student does not meet the requirements of § 49-4-905(b)(2). To be eligible under this section, the student shall:

(1) Graduate from a high school in the foreign nation where the student's parent is a religious worker that is accredited by a regional accrediting association as defined by § 49-4-902 and meet the academic eligibility requirements of § 49-4-907(3); or

(2) Complete high school in a home school in the foreign nation where the student's parent is a religious worker and meet the academic eligibility requirements of § 49-4-908(2)(A).

(b) As used in this section:

(1) "Dependent child" means a natural or adopted child or stepchild whom the parent who is a religious worker claims as a dependent for federal income tax purposes; provided, however, that the child is under twenty-one (21) years of age and resides in another nation only while the parent is actively engaged in full-time religious work; and

(2) "Religious worker" means a person sent to another country by a church, religious denomination or other religious organization to spread its faith or to do social or medical work.

(c) This section shall only apply to dependent children of religious workers who are engaged in full-time religious work in another nation for more than one (1) year and who were Tennessee residents before leaving the United States to do religious work and intend to return to Tennessee upon completion of their assignment as a religious worker.

49-6-2907.   Voluntary participation of personnel in religious activities on school grounds.

(a) LEAs and school administrators may not prohibit personnel from participating in religious activities on school grounds that are initiated by students at reasonable times before or after the instructional day so long as such activities are voluntary for all parties and do not conflict with the responsibilities or assignments of such personnel.

(b) Nothing in this section shall prohibit LEAs and school administrators from allowing personnel to participate in other constitutionally permissible religious activities on school grounds.

49-7-156.   No discrimination or denial of recognition to student organization on basis of religious content of organization's speech -- Restricting membership to persons professing the faith of the group is allowed.

(a) No state higher education institution that grants recognition to any student organization shall discriminate against or deny recognition to a student organization, or deny to a student organization access to programs, funding, or facilities otherwise available to another student organization, on the basis of:

(1) The religious content of the organization's speech including, but not limited to, worship; or

(2) The organization's exercise of its rights pursuant to subsection (b).

(b) A religious student organization may determine that the organization's religious mission requires that only persons professing the faith of the group and comporting themselves in conformity with it qualify to serve as members or leaders.

(c) As used in this section, "state higher education institution" means any higher education institution governed by chapter 8 or 9 of this title.

68-34-104. Contraceptives -- Availability -- Information -- Religious belief.

It is the policy and authority of this state that:

(1) All medically acceptable contraceptive procedures, supplies, and information shall be readily and practicably available to each and every person desirous of the same regardless of sex, race, age, income, number of children, marital status, citizenship or motive;

(2) Contraceptive procedures, including medical procedures for permanent sterilization, when performed by a physician on a requesting and consenting patient, are consistent with public policy;

(3) Nothing in this chapter shall inhibit a physician from refusing to furnish any contraceptive procedures, supplies or information where such refusal is for medical reasons;

(4) Dissemination of medically acceptable contraceptive information by duly authorized persons in state and county health and welfare departments, in medical facilities at institutions of higher learning, and at other agencies and instrumentalities of this state is consistent with public policy;

(5) No private institution or physician, nor any agent or employee of such institution or physician, shall be prohibited from refusing to provide contraceptive procedures, supplies, and information when such refusal is based upon religious or conscientious objection, and no such institution, employee, agent, or physician shall be

held liable for such refusal; and

(6) To the extent that family planning funds are available, each public health agency of this state and each of its political subdivisions shall provide contraceptive procedures, supplies, and information, including voluntary sterilization procedures for male or female persons eligible for free medical service as determined by rules and regulations promulgated by the commissioner. The same service shall be available to all others who are unable to obtain the service privately, at a cost to be determined by rules and regulations promulgated by the commissioner.

57-5-109. Proximity to schools, churches, places of public gatherings.

(a) A city or county shall not suspend, revoke or deny a permit to a business engaged in selling, distributing or manufacturing beer on the basis of the proximity of the business to a school, residence, church, or other place of public gathering if a valid permit had been issued to any business on that same location. This section shall not apply if beer is not sold, distributed or manufactured at that location during any continuous six-month period.

(b) For the purposes of this section, "on that same location" means within the boundaries of the parcel or tract of the real property on which the business was located. This section applies whether or not a business moves the building on the location and whether or not the business was a conforming or nonconforming use at the time of the move.

(c) If a business applies for a beer permit within the continuous six-month period referenced in this section, and if the city or county denies the business a permit and if the business appeals that denial, a new six-month continuous sale period shall begin to run on the date when the appeal of that denial is final.

Appendix 3

Weapons Laws Relevant to Religious Institutions in Kentucky

Verification of the accuracy is advised as laws frequently change.

Some of the content not pertaining specifically to churches and faith organizations or members is not included but the sections may be listed intentionally without content.

237.115 Construction of KRS 237.110 -- Prohibition by local government units of carrying concealed deadly weapons in governmental buildings --Restriction on criminal penalties.

(1) Except as provided in KRS 527.020, nothing contained in KRS 237.110 shall be construed to limit, restrict, or prohibit in any manner the right of a college, university, or any postsecondary education facility, including technical schools and community colleges, to control the possession of deadly weapons on any property owned or controlled by them or the right of a unit of state, city, county, urban-county, or charter county government to prohibit the carrying of concealed deadly weapons by licensees in that portion of a building actually owned, leased, or occupied by that unit of government.

(2) Except as provided in KRS 527.020, the legislative body of a state, city, county, or urban-county government may, by statute, administrative regulation, or ordinance, prohibit or limit the carrying of concealed deadly weapons by licensees in that portion of a building owned, leased, or

controlled by that unit of government. That portion of a building in which the carrying of concealed deadly weapons is prohibited or limited shall be clearly identified by signs posted at the entrance to the restricted area. The statute or ordinance shall exempt any building used for public housing by private persons, highway rest areas, firing ranges, and private dwellings owned, leased, or controlled by that unit of government from any restriction on the carrying or possession of deadly weapons. The statute, administrative regulation, or ordinance shall not specify any criminal penalty for its violation but may specify that persons violating the statute or ordinance may be denied entrance to the building, ordered to leave the building, and if employees of the unit of government, be subject to employee disciplinary measures for violation of the provisions of the statute or ordinance. The provisions of this section shall not be deemed to be a violation of KRS 65.870 if the requirements of this section are followed. The provisions of this section shall not apply to any other unit of government.

(3) Unless otherwise specifically provided by the Kentucky Revised Statutes or applicable federal law, no criminal penalty shall attach to carrying a concealed firearm or other deadly weapon with a permit at any location at which an unconcealed firearm or other deadly weapon may be constitutionally carried.

527.020 Carrying concealed deadly weapon. (Effective as of July 15, 2014)

(In Part)

(1) A person is guilty of carrying a concealed weapon when he or she carries concealed a firearm or other deadly weapon on or about his or her person.

(2) Peace officers and certified court security officers, when necessary for their protection in the discharge of their official duties; United States mail carriers when

actually engaged in their duties; and agents and messengers of express companies, when necessary for their protection in the discharge of their official duties, may carry concealed weapons on or about their person.

(3) The director of the Division of Law Enforcement in the Department of Fish and Wildlife Resources, conservation officers of the Department of Fish and Wildlife Resources, and policemen directly employed by state, county, city, or urban-county governments may carry concealed deadly weapons on or about their person at all times within the Commonwealth of Kentucky, when expressly authorized to do so by law or by the government employing the officer.

(4) Persons, except those specified in subsection (5) of this section, licensed to carry a concealed deadly weapon pursuant to KRS 237.110 may carry a firearm or other concealed deadly weapon on or about their persons at all times within the Commonwealth of Kentucky, if the firearm or concealed deadly weapon is carried in conformity with the requirements of that section. Unless otherwise specifically provided by the Kentucky Revised Statutes or applicable federal law, no criminal penalty shall attach to carrying a concealed firearm or other deadly weapon with a permit at any location at which an unconcealed firearm or other deadly weapon may be constitutionally carried. No person or organization, public or private, shall prohibit a person licensed to carry a concealed deadly weapon from possessing a firearm, ammunition, or both, or other deadly weapon in his or her vehicle in compliance with the provisions of KRS 237.110 and 237.115. Any attempt by a person or organization, public or private, to violate the provisions of this subsection may be the subject of an action for appropriate relief or for damages in a Circuit Court or District Court of competent jurisdiction.

(Additional followed but did not change the meaning of this area.)

Appendix 4

Weapons Laws Relevant to Religious Institutions in Texas

Sec. 46.035. UNLAWFUL CARRYING OF HANDGUN BY LICENSE HOLDER.

(a) A license holder commits an offense if the license holder carries a handgun on or about the license holder's person under the authority of Subchapter H, Chapter 411, Government Code, and intentionally displays the handgun in plain view of another person in a public place.

(b) A license holder commits an offense if the license holder intentionally, knowingly, or recklessly carries a handgun under the authority of Subchapter H, Chapter 411, Government Code, regardless of whether the handgun is concealed, on or about the license holder's person:

(1) on the premises of a business that has a permit or license issued under Chapter 25, 28, 32, 69, or 74, Alcoholic Beverage Code, if the business derives 51 percent or more of its income from the sale or service of alcoholic beverages for on-premises consumption, as determined by the Texas Alcoholic Beverage Commission under Section 104.06, Alcoholic Beverage Code;

(2) on the premises where a high school, collegiate, or professional sporting event or interscholastic event is taking place, unless the license holder is a participant in the event and a handgun is used in the event;

(3) on the premises of a correctional facility;

(4) on the premises of a hospital licensed under Chapter 241, Health and Safety Code, or on the premises of a nursing home licensed under Chapter 242, Health and Safety Code, unless the license holder has written authorization of the hospital or nursing home administration, as appropriate;

(5) in an amusement park; or

(6) on the premises of a church, synagogue, or other established place of religious worship.

Sec. 46.15. NONAPPLICABILITY.

(a) Sections 46.02 and 46.03 do not apply to:

(1) peace officers or special investigators under Article 2.122, Code of Criminal Procedure, and neither section prohibits a peace officer or special investigator from carrying a weapon in this state, including in an establishment in this state serving the public, regardless of whether the peace officer or special investigator is engaged in the actual discharge of the officer's or investigator's duties while carrying the weapon;

(2) parole officers and neither section prohibits an officer from carrying a weapon in this state if the officer is:

(A) engaged in the actual discharge of the officer's duties while carrying the weapon; and

(B) in compliance with policies and procedures adopted by the Texas Department of Criminal Justice regarding the possession of a weapon by an officer while on duty;

(3) community supervision and corrections department officers appointed or employed under Section

76.004, Government Code, and neither section prohibits an officer from carrying a weapon in this state if the officer is:

(A) engaged in the actual discharge of the officer's duties while carrying the weapon; and

(B) authorized to carry a weapon under Section 76.0051, Government Code;

(4) an active judicial officer as defined by Section 411.201, Government Code, who is licensed to carry a concealed handgun under Subchapter H, Chapter 411, Government Code;

(5) an honorably retired peace officer, qualified retired law enforcement officer, federal criminal investigator, or former reserve law enforcement officer who holds a certificate of proficiency issued under Section 1701.357, Occupations Code, and is carrying a photo identification that is issued by a federal, state, or local law enforcement agency, as applicable, and that verifies that the officer is:

(A) an honorably retired peace officer;

(B) a qualified retired law enforcement officer;

(C) a federal criminal investigator; or

(D) a former reserve law enforcement officer who has served in that capacity not less than a total of 15 years with one or more state or local law enforcement agencies;

(6) a district attorney, criminal district attorney, county attorney, or municipal attorney who is licensed to carry a concealed handgun under Subchapter H, Chapter 411, Government Code;

(7) an assistant district attorney, assistant criminal district attorney, or assistant county attorney who is

licensed to carry a concealed handgun under Subchapter H, Chapter 411, Government Code;

(8) a bailiff designated by an active judicial officer as defined by Section 411.201, Government Code, who is:

(A) licensed to carry a concealed handgun under Chapter 411, Government Code; and

(B) engaged in escorting the judicial officer; or

(9) a juvenile probation officer who is authorized to carry a firearm under Section 142.006, Human Resources Code.

(b) Section 46.02 does not apply to a person who:

(1) is in the actual discharge of official duties as a member of the armed forces or state military forces as defined by Section 437.001, Government Code, or as a guard employed by a penal institution;

(2) is traveling;

(3) is engaging in lawful hunting, fishing, or other sporting activity on the immediate premises where the activity is conducted, or is en route between the premises and the actor's residence, motor vehicle, or watercraft, if the weapon is a type commonly used in the activity;

(4) holds a security officer commission issued by the Texas Private Security Board, if the person is engaged in the performance of the person's duties as an officer commissioned under Chapter 1702, Occupations Code, or is traveling to or from the person's place of assignment and is wearing the officer's uniform and carrying the officer's weapon in plain view;

(5) acts as a personal protection officer and carries

the person's security officer commission and personal protection officer authorization, if the person:

(A) is engaged in the performance of the person's duties as a personal protection officer under Chapter 1702, Occupations Code, or is traveling to or from the person's place of assignment; and

(B) is either:

(i) wearing the uniform of a security officer, including any uniform or apparel described by Section 1702.323(d), Occupations Code, and carrying the officer's weapon in plain view; or

(ii) not wearing the uniform of a security officer and carrying the officer's weapon in a concealed manner;

(6) is carrying a concealed handgun and a valid license issued under Subchapter H, Chapter 411, Government Code, to carry a concealed handgun;

(7) holds an alcoholic beverage permit or license or is an employee of a holder of an alcoholic beverage permit or license if the person is supervising the operation of the permitted or licensed premises; or

(8) is a student in a law enforcement class engaging in an activity required as part of the class, if the weapon is a type commonly used in the activity and the person is:

(A) on the immediate premises where the activity is conducted; or

(B) en route between those premises and the person's residence and is carrying the weapon unloaded.

(c) The provision of Section 46.02 prohibiting the carrying of a club does not apply to a noncommissioned security guard at an institution of higher education who carries a nightstick or similar club, and who has undergone 15 hours of training in the proper use of the club, including at least seven hours of training in the use of the club for nonviolent restraint. For the purposes of this subsection, "nonviolent restraint" means the use of reasonable force, not intended and not likely to inflict bodily injury.

(d) The provisions of Section 46.02 prohibiting the carrying of a firearm or carrying of a club do not apply to a public security officer employed by the adjutant general under Section 437.053, Government Code, in performance of official duties or while traveling to or from a place of duty.

(e) The provisions of Section 46.02 prohibiting the carrying of an illegal knife do not apply to an individual carrying a bowie knife or a sword used in a historical demonstration or in a ceremony in which the knife or sword is significant to the performance of the ceremony.

(f) Section 46.03(a)(6) does not apply to a person who possesses a firearm or club while in the actual discharge of official duties as:

(1) a member of the armed forces or state military forces, as defined by Section 437.001, Government Code; or

(2) an employee of a penal institution.

(g) The provisions of Sections 46.02 and 46.03 prohibiting the possession or carrying of a club do not apply to an animal control officer who holds a certificate issued under Section 829.006, Health and Safety Code, and who possesses or carries an instrument used specifically for deterring the bite of an animal while the officer is in the performance of official duties under the Health and Safety Code or is traveling to or from a place of duty.

Sec. 411.203.   Rights of Employers. This subchapter

does not prevent or otherwise limit the right of a public or private employer to prohibit persons who are licensed under this subchapter from carrying a concealed handgun on the premises of the business. In this section, "premises" has the meaning assigned by Section 46.035(f)(3), Penal Code.

Sec. 30.06. TRESPASS BY HOLDER OF LICENSE TO CARRY CONCEALED HANDGUN.

(a) A license holder commits an offense if the license holder:

> (1) carries a handgun under the authority of Subchapter H, Chapter 411, Government Code, on property of another without effective consent; and

> (2) received notice that:

>> (A) entry on the property by a license holder with a concealed handgun was forbidden; or

>> (B) remaining on the property with a concealed handgun was forbidden and failed to depart.

(b) For purposes of this section, a person receives notice if the owner of the property or someone with apparent authority to act for the owner provides notice to the person by oral or written communication.

(c) In this section:

> (1) "Entry" has the meaning assigned by Section 30.05(b).

> (2) "License holder" has the meaning assigned by Section 46.035(f).

> (3) "Written communication" means:

>> (A) a card or other document on which is written language identical to the following: "Pursuant to Section 30.06, Penal Code (trespass by holder of license to carry a concealed handgun), a person

licensed under Subchapter H, Chapter 411, Government Code (concealed handgun law), may not enter this property with a concealed handgun"; or

(B) a sign posted on the property that:

(i) includes the language described by Paragraph (A) in both English and Spanish;

(ii) appears in contrasting colors with block letters at least one inch in height; and

(iii) is displayed in a conspicuous manner clearly visible to the public.

Appendix 5

Security Team Special Instructions (Suggestions)

Your assignment is at the side entrance to the auditorium. This is your control point for all incidents which may occur. Stay near this exit from the beginning of your usher assignment until the service is concluded and congregants have left the auditorium.

In the event of:

<u>Medical emergency</u> –

- Summon on-call medical help immediately (see list). Call 911 if directed by _____.

- If life threatening condition appears to be present, interrupt service by saying, "Excuse me, – I need a doctor right away."

- Lend assistance to victim and then to medical responders as needed.

- Do NOT administer first aid for which you have not been trained, except under supervision of trained medical personnel (i.e. assisting with CPR, etc.)

<u>Evacuation for Threats</u> (Fire, Bomb, other) – upon announcement from the Minister or Designee

- Take position at this exit door

- Prevent entry of unauthorized persons

- Take charge of evacuation through this exit.

- Send other usher(s) or trusted congregant(s) to

other exit doors if needed to assist orderly evacuation.

- Tell people "Don't Run; Go to _____; Assist those around you" – Repeat these instructions calmly and clearly, slowly and constantly.

Emergency evacuation for Actual Fire, Explosion or incident –

- Take same steps as described in Evacuation for Threats above, and

- Try to keep order during emergency evacuations – your very presence there with calming, clear instructions can do this.

- Repeat these instructions calmly and clearly, slowly and constantly.

- If smoke or dust is in the air, tell people to bend down and keep low as they move.

- If possible, send other usher(s) or trusted congregant(s) to other exit doors if needed.

Violent attack with weapons – (Active Shooter)

- If the perpetrator is not in the building, in sight or an imminent danger those with responsible charge must determine if hiding (sheltering in place) is the best option.

- If sheltering is not the best option due to the perpetrator being on the move and safe escape is possible, try to assist people exiting.

- If evacuation is not possible and movement is not possible, tell people to "Get down" and "Get on the floor." In most instances an active shooter starts suddenly and this may be the best option if shots are being fired within the auditorium.

- On the floor is also where congregants (and you) need to be if armed police enter to confront the intruders.

- If confronted by armed attackers, do as you are ordered and try to keep them calm. Do not be confrontational or belligerent when your personal safety and that of others may be at risk.

- If you have sheltered and the shooter is entering your sheltered or hiding area, be prepared and committed to fight with as much force as you can muster to save yourself and others. Use heavy items as weapons and attempt to incapacitate the perpetrator to allow for escape. (Each organization's leadership must develop policies and plans that reflect their beliefs and what is authorized regarding fighting as a last resort.)

The most recent trend in these situations is to uses the easy to remember progression of "Run, Hide, Fight."

1. Run from the danger while telling others of the danger and preventing their entering the area if possible.

2. Hide if possible and time does not allow for a complete escape.

3. Fight as a last resort and commit to continue fighting until safe escape is possible, the perpetrator is incapacitated, or is restrained.

Appendix 6

Weapons Situations

Specifics

1. Assess the situation.

2. Notify police. Provide as much information as possible. Be prepared to act as a resource and liaison between church and police. If necessary, have a map of the building available for police.

3. Gather as much detailed information as possible. Try to determine:

   - Location, identity and detailed description of individual.

   - Location and description of weapon.

   - Any pertinent background information on individual, including possible reason for carrying a weapon.

4. Isolate individual or suspect. (If weapon is in a car or elsewhere, prevent access to it.)

5. If interaction with the individual is imminent, avoid sudden moves or gestures.

6. Remain calm. Try not to raise your voice -- but, if this becomes necessary, do so decisively and with clarity. Your tone and demeanor will strongly influence the outcome of the crisis.

7. Use emergency signal to notify others of the threatening situation and have them keep others away until all is clear.

Handling a Weapon-Wielding Subject

- Evacuate the area
- Evaluate the perpetrator
- Isolate
- Negotiate
- Remain calm
- Get help
- Avoid heroics
- Don't threaten
- Keep a safe, non-intimidating distance
- Avoid abrupt sporadic movements
- Look for a place to dive or jump
- Report incident to law enforcement

(Adapted from National School Safety Center)

Appendix 7

Preventing Church HVAC Theft

Criminals often prey on those who provide easy opportunities that ensure them they are less likely to be detected or encounter substantial resistance. Criminals choose their victims based upon: the amount of the reward, the amount of effort required and the degree of risk anticipated. Recently the trend toward the theft of copper and aluminum has extended to homes that may be vacant during the day, offices and even churches. Churches in have seen an increase in victimization over the last several months. Ministers and congregants are finding entire heat pumps missing when they arrive to worship. Why, you ask, most estimates indicate that the price of copper has tripled over a few short years. A quick trip to the scrap yard can net the thief rich dividends for his criminal work.

What can be done to address these crime problems? The criminal justice system needs to react quickly. But the prevention and intervention steps will require more than just the police. The Institute of Scrap Recycling Industries Inc. (ISRI) has published documents for recyclers that encourage them to work with local law enforcement officials to share information. The suggested process includes law enforcement alerts to recyclers when thefts occur, with descriptions of what items may be offered for sale. Recently ISRI has created a tool for law enforcement that allows officers to alert the scrap industry of significant thefts of materials in the United States and Canada.

While voluntary cooperation is always desired, some

state laws provides law enforcement specific tools to head off this phenomenon by mandating certain processes with regard to scrap metal.

There are other techniques to help limit the opportunity for the theft of copper and aluminum wiring and pipes. To prevent the stripping of air conditioning units of their copper coils, property owners may enclose their unit in a wire cage or padlock their power disconnect box with a quality disc type padlock. This type of lock makes it difficult, if not impossible to cut the lock. Home improvement stores offer many brands of these locks for under $20. If this is more important to the church it may opt to purchase a commercially available product Copper Watcher™ which monitors the A/C systems and acts similarly to an alarm company. This company may be contacted at:

www.copperwatcher.com

Other recommendations include securing crawl spaces with access to pipes and wiring, increasing the security of housings and coverings with tamper resistant screws, leaving the electric current on in vacated buildings, leaving certain lights on and making law enforcement officials aware of the building's status.

Anything that can be done to limit the reward and make the theft more difficult will substantially reduce the probability of victimization. Local crime prevention practitioners and law enforcement officers, sound prevention techniques, and state laws are all essential to creating a coordinated, effective barrier to church HVAC theft.

Appendix 8

Benevolence Cons and Abusers

The church is instructed to be benevolent in assisting certain groups of persons and even other congregations. Understanding that there may be some dispute of who the church treasury may support or even who the individual Christians should assist, we must agree that at least some benevolence is expected from the church. "As we have therefore opportunity, let us do good unto all *men*, especially unto them who are of the household of faith." Gal. 6:10 (Also 1 Tim. 5:9-16, Acts 2:44-45, 4:34-37 and 6:1-8) Regardless of what is commanded, if a church sees need to assist members through benevolence we must do it wisely.

The scriptures teach that we are to be "good stewards" of all the Lord provides. (Luke 12:42-49, 1 Cor. 4:1-2, 1 Pet. 4:10, et. al.) In order to create an environment conducive to efficient operation of the church treasury while meeting the needs of those seeking benevolence for hardships guidance should be established.

For the purpose of this discussion, we are assuming that at least some support is provided to non-members, travelers, members in emergency situations and so on. Most requests will be relative to the following:

✓ Utility Payments (Electricity, fuel oil, water, natural gas, etc.)

✓ Rent or Mortgage Payment assistance

✓ Automobile repair/fuel assistance

✓ Travel Lodging

✓ Food assistance

✓ Clothing (specifically essential clothing such as coats in cold weather)

✓ Prescription or other verified medical need (Glasses and dental only for emergency or dire cases)

In order to guide in this distribution and to avoid most issues men must be appointed to oversee this work and a policy guiding them will be helpful to avoid arguments and accusations of favoritism as found in Acts 6, mentioned above. A policy will also give the member receiving the call so information that they may share which in the long run will eliminate some illegitimate requests and even cons.

Identifying A Scam/Abuse

First let's consider the con artists, scammers or thieves that perpetrate these crimes. Those working in the field of crime prevention understand that all scams operate on the church's desire to assist those in need. Scammers and abusers are relying on the church to not have a policy, to not verify the need, to not verify accuracy of the information given, and to not delay in giving. They try to guarantee that by timing their requests. That is the first red flag!

The scammers who are "frequent flyers" are most likely to show up at the church just before 5:00 p.m. on Friday or on a holiday when the offices that the church might verify their story with will be closed. This is also the case when a person shows up on a Sunday morning but more likely a Sunday night service to ask for assistance for a broken down car, travel expenses etc. The idea is that regardless of what they tell you, you can't verify it. If they say their electricity was turned off and they have a sick child, you can't pay the bill directly for them and, rather than be inconvenienced, some churches fork out the cash. The alleged member of the church in some other state shows up on Sunday night, just before services to request assistance and you can't verify the person is a member or not of the church they claim membership at. Additionally, the church may not be able to verify the need.

Scammers and abusers usually seek cash but that does not mean that they will not also scam through other means. In some cases, the need, such as travel lodging may be verifiable by the person asking if the church can pay for a room for the night. The room may have indeed been needed and the church avoided giving cash but the individual may just be traveling on vacation and letting the church foot the bill.

In other cases people who do not see what they are doing as scamming may be local residents, abusers. They may go church to church to pay their bills so that they can use their cash or other sources of income to purchase illicit drugs, alcohol and items that they cannot with their food stamps. In some cases these are individuals who have fallen into the dependency plan of living. They simply take advantage of anything they can get for free, whether they are truly in need or not. They are just as guilty of obtaining money by false pretenses as the traveling scammer. They will frequently alternate from church to church or denomination to denomination, until they come back around and start all over. These scammers eventually get identified by churches which no longer fall prey to their alleged needs and refuse to assist them.

Reducing the Scam Possibility

We have identified some key red flags but why not go beyond that and apply situational crime prevention techniques to the problem in policy guidance. When drafting a policy we want to guide those overseeing this work in:

1. Mitigating any scammed loss amounts,

2. Increasing the effort required for the scammer to have success,

3. Removing any excuses the scammer may have for not providing what is needed for assistance, and

4. Increasing the perceived risk that they will be identified as attempting a scam.

The first thing any congregation should understand is that the church's priority is to seek and save the lost. In being true to the work of evangelism, and understanding that funding is limited, we *must* be good stewards of whatever funds are available. That means that we should not provide funds without ensuring the legitimacy of the needs. That means that we should not provide for needs for which tax dollars have already established a means for assisting with and most certainly that means that we should not provide for those that *choose* to be destitute. *"For even when we were with you, this we commanded you, that if any would not work, neither should he eat."* (2 Thess. 3:10) The church policy should clearly give preference to helping those who are of the household of faith first. *"For if any provide not for his own, and specially for those of his own house, he hath denied the faith, and is worse than an infidel."* (1 Tim. 5:8)

So how do we accomplish the four crime prevention items in policy? Let's look at some items that, if included, go a long way to accomplishing these and thus prevention of scams.

The policy should identify what benevolence

requests will be considered.

<u>Example:</u>

The church leadership shall identify a minimum of two men to oversee the requests for benevolence and apply this policy guidance in determining any assistance to be provided.

a. For the purpose of this policy benevolence assistance requests shall include primarily the following:

1. Utility Payments (Electricity, fuel oil, water, natural gas, etc.)

2. Rent or Mortgage Payment assistance

3. Automobile repair/fuel assistance

4. Travel Lodging

5. Food assistance

6. Clothing (specifically essential clothing such as coats in cold weather)

7. Prescription or other verified medical need (Glasses and dental only for emergency or dire cases)

The policy should clearly identify who is responsible for making benevolence decisions and how requests will be received. The minister should not be given this responsibility as it may interfere with his other duties and removes the time and distance needed to make a sound decision with regard to benevolence.

<u>Example</u>

This policy shall guide in providing requests from outside entities (non-members of the local church) and shall not specifically apply to members of the local congregation in need.

a. All requests for assistance must be made in person to the Elders or Deacons in conjunction with a regular meeting of the church. (Bible class, Worship Service, Fellowship etc.) [No criminal likes to be under scrutiny and this requirement alone contributes to increasing the perceived risk of future identification.]

b. Upon receiving a request, the Minister (or any other receiving the request) shall advise the caller (requestor) of the policy that they must meet the men appointed over this work prior to any assistance being approved or offered. The individual receiving the request will ask if they want to meet on (the next appointed meeting time) and invite the caller to participate in the meeting prior. If they schedule to be there, the men appointed over this work shall be notified in advance of the expected presence and the nature of the request. [As mentioned above the criminals seek timing that is beneficial to them, this policy requirement puts the timing advantage back with the church and increases the efforts for the criminal to be successful.]

c. The men appointed over this work shall complete a record of the request on a form devised to be provided at the next regular Business Meeting for retention and accounting purposes. The men over this work shall make a decision in accordance with the remainder of this policy.

   i. The requestor shall be given the decision by telephone later, when not an emergency to be done that day. This will allow the men to discuss the issue privately and will eliminate potential anger outbursts from any denial. [This aspect of the policy provides protection from violence but more, it provides the advantage to the church members to avoid intimidation.]

   ii. Once a decision is made to assist, one of the men will notify the Treasurer of where and to whom to make payment via check, credit card, debit card, or personal funds to be reimbursed by the church. *No cash or check will be given an individual requesting funds directly. [Again, this increases the efforts for the criminal scammer.]

   ii. *The men shall give a report on the authorized benevolence at the next financial report meeting.*

  d. At no time shall the men knowingly exceed the budget for benevolence without discussion and consideration among leadership. [This is the first step in mitigating and limiting losses.]

The policy should provide specific guidance in handling the various requests to ensure that all other public avenues of assistance have been exhausted and that the need is legitimate. The church should do their homework in advance and have a listing of as many available local taxpayer funded resources to assist in providing assistance with these needs. The policy should also identify the maximum amounts, absent extenuating circumstances, that the men over this work will be authorized arrange payment of. [These specific amounts further mitigate losses and in some cases the amounts are insufficient to the criminal for the risk, thus eliminating the church as a target.]

Example

155

Utility Payments

a. Any request for assistance must reveal that other means of assistance have been exhausted. The men will request to see an overdue, or shut-off notice. If the need is verified by the men appointed over this work, a onetime payment of up to $XXX.XX shall be authorized to be made directly to the utility company to assist in sustaining or restoring the service. When the amount is substantially higher than the church policy authorizes, the requestor will be encouraged to obtain assistance in part from others first. They will be informed of the policy limitations, as well as our desire to assist. The men will offer to pay the policy authorized amount once they can confirm the remaining amount has been pledged payment (from the utility company or other paying source.)

A copy of the bill with the account number must be provided the treasurer and he may then draft a check paying that amount.

Rent or Mortgage Payment assistance

a. Any request for assistance must assert that other means of assistance have been exhausted. The men may choose to contact the landlord or review a notice of overdue rent/payment. If the need is verified by the men appointed over this work, a onetime payment of up to $XXX.XX shall be authorized to be made directly to the rental agent or lending institution. A copy of the bill/notice with the account number must be provided the treasurer and he may then draft a check paying that amount.

Automobile repair/automobile fuel assistance

a. Any request for assistance must provide an estimate of repair from a local shop that can be verified. Only repairs of a mechanical necessity will be covered. No cosmetic or non-essential repairs will be paid. If the need is verified by the men appointed over this work, assistance for repair in the amount of up to $XXX.XX shall be authorized to be made directly to the repair company. A copy of the bill with the account number must be provided the treasurer and he may then draft a check paying that amount.

b. If automobile fuel assistance is requested information must be provided the men as to destination, purpose of travel, and other questions they may have. Assistance, not to exceed $XX.XX may be provided and the men may accompany the requestor to a gasoline fueling station and pay directly from their account. They may turn in the receipt to the Treasurer who will reimburse them for the fuel assistance.

Travel Lodging

a. Any request for emergency lodging assistance must assert that other means of assistance have been exhausted. The men will attempt to verify the need and absence of family or other resources. (i.e. car broken down and expending all cash for repairs that will take overnight, domestic abuse, evicted from residence, etc.) If the need is verified by the men appointed over this work, a one night's lodging payment shall be authorized in an amount not to exceed $XXXX.XX to be paid directly to the motel. To expedite this, the Treasurer may call and pay for the room on the church credit card, debit card or pay by other means. A copy of the receipt will be retained for the church records.

Food assistance

a. Should the church have sufficient food in the food pantry all requests will first be addressed by authorizing those requesting assistance with food needs to obtain food stuffs from the pantry first.

b. In the absence of a food pantry, the men will verify the need and will provide assistance not to exceed $XX.XX per household member. (4 members=$XXX.XX) for a onetime assistance. The men or other members who are available will accompany the requestor to the grocery and will pay for the essential groceries, excluding items such as; candy, cookies, pet food, lottery tickets, alcohol, and tobacco products. The receipt will be turned in to the Treasurer with the assistance information for a full reimbursement.

Clothing (specifically essential clothing such as coats in cold weather)

a. Any request for assistance must assert that other means of assistance have been exhausted. Should the church have at its disposal a "clothes closet for the needy" program, the requestor will first be directed to this resource. The men may then accompany the needy to the Goodwill or other discount store to seek appropriate clothing, if the need is verified by the men appointed over this work, a purchase of the clothing may be authorized in an amount not to exceed $XX.XX. A copy of the receipt will be provided the treasurer for reimbursement.

Prescription or other verified medical need (Glasses and dental only for emergency or dire cases)

a. Any request for medical assistance must be an emergency matter and all other means of assistance must have been exhausted. The local emergency room turns no emergencies away. Several programs exist for assistance for glasses and dentistry and these, being non-essentials shall not be addressed by the church. (See the list of local free services available to the indigent)

b. If all means for coverage of an essential prescription are exhausted, the men may then accompany the requestor to the pharmacy and pay for the prescription (generic) and turn in the receipt for reimbursement.

Any amounts paid exceeding those allowed in this policy must be authorized by consulting the Elders or in the absence of the Elders, the Deacons and the Treasurer.

These sorts of policies have reduced scams and abusers at the point of contact when they call the church office and are told that they need to meet with the men over the work first and that a policy of benevolence is in place. Only those with legitimate needs are likely to make the meeting. Those with these policies have seen some say they would be there but not arrive. Those that attend the meetings are most often deemed legitimate and provided assistance. Some however were determined at the meetings to be trying to get funding that they did not need and, once denied, they rarely return seeking illegitimate assistance.

Some seem opposed to implementing these policies, just as they do not see security as a need. I would suggest that as a result of these policies, the church is better able to fund legitimate needs and to be good stewards.

Presentations

Brother Arrington provides presentations outside of Virginia for a reasonable fee to cover time, travel and expenses.

All inquiries for presentations or to order copies of this book should be sent to the e-mail of Armor1@centurylink.net.

NOTES:

CPSIA information can be obtained
at www.ICGtesting.com
Printed in the USA
FFOW03n1740221117
43611670-42421FF